WHISKEY

MICHAEL DIETSCH

WHISKEY

A SPIRITED STORY WITH
75 CLASSIC & ORIGINAL COCKTAILS

THE COUNTRYMAN PRESS
A division of W. W. Norton & Company
Independent Publishers Since 1923

For information about permission to reproduce selections from this book,
write to Permissions, The Countryman Press, 500 Fifth Avenue, New York, NY 10110

For information about special discounts for bulk purchases, please contact
W. W. Norton Special Sales at specialsales@wwnorton.com or 800-233-4830

The Countryman Press
www.countrymanpress.com

A division of W. W. Norton & Company, Inc.
500 Fifth Avenue, New York, NY 10110
www.wwnorton.com

Library of Congress Cataloging-in-Publication Data

Names: Dietsch, Michael, author.
Title: Whiskey : a spirited story with 75 classic and original cocktails /
   Michael Dietsch.
Description: Woodstock, VT : The Countryman Press, a division of
W.W. Norton & Company, [2016] | Includes index.
Identifiers: LCCN 2015044032 | ISBN 9781581573251 (hardcover)
Subjects: LCSH: Cocktails. | Whiskey. | LCGFT: Cookbooks.
Classification: LCC TX951 .D5155 2016 | DDC 641.2/52—dc23
LC record available at http://lccn.loc.gov/2015044032

10 9 8 7 6 5 4 3 2 1

To my parents: Patricia, who doesn't drink whiskey,
and Virgil, who did

ACKNOWLEDGMENTS

Writing a book is at times a sprint and at other times a marathon. I want to thank Ann Treistman and the team at Countryman Press and Norton, including Sarah Bennett; production whizzes Devon Zahn and Natalie Eilbert; and copy editor Diane Durrett. Thanks, too, to cover photographer Kristy Gardner. I again especially want to thank Nick Caruso for his beautiful design. Nick's done a wonderful job on this book and both editions of my first book, *Shrubs,* and I couldn't be happier.

I want to thank my publicists, Jill Browning and Devorah Backman, for helping me get the word out about *Shrubs.* The book reached a wider audience than I ever envisioned, and I owe much of its success to them.

Many thanks again to my agent, Vicky Bijur, for her warmth, wisdom, and tireless advocacy.

Several of the interviews and photographs stemmed from a Spring 2015 trip along the American Whiskey Trail, hosted by the Distilled Spirits Council of the United States (DISCUS). I want to thank everyone at DISCUS, especially Alexandra Sklansky, who coordinated the trip. Many thanks as well to Greg Davis, Chris Morris, Eddie Russell, and Fred Noe—all of whom answered questions I had about the history and processes of making good whiskey.

For their contributions, inspiration, and encouragement, I want to thank Brooks Baldwin, Meriko Borogove, Paul Clarke, Camper English, Andrew Friedman, Ted Haigh, Robert and Nancy Hess, Maggie Hoffman, Lindsey Johnson, Adam Lantheaume, Hanna Lee, Jeffrey Morgenthaler, Lauren Mote, Matthew Rowley, Manuela Savona, Robert Simonson, Chuck Taggart, Sean Timberlake, Keith Waldbauer, and David Wondrich.

My kids, Julian and Mirabelle, are a constant inspiration, if mainly to spur me to sell enough books to keep their toy box well stocked. My wife, Jennifer Hess, was again the photographer for these recipes, spending much of her weekends shooting and styling and coaxing, all the while helping wrangle the aforementioned children. Jen, sweetheart, you are done! Thanks for seeing me across the finish line.

CONTENTS

INTRODUCTION
11

Chapter 1
WHAT IS WHISKEY?
15

Chapter 2
INTRODUCTION TO INTERNATIONAL WHISKEY
41

Chapter 3
HOW TO MAKE A COCKTAIL
75

Chapter 4
HISTORIC WHISKEY COCKTAILS
95

1860–1899: The First Golden Age of the Cocktail
112

1900–1920: Pre-Prohibition Whiskey Cocktails
138

1920–1933: Prohibition-Era Whiskey Cocktails
153

1933–1999: Post-Prohibition Whiskey Cocktails
171

2000–Today: Cocktail Renaissance, or the Second Golden Age of the Cocktail
191

Chapter 5
MIXER RECIPES
203

INDEX
212

INTRODUCTION

On a mild day in the spring of 2014, I stood on a bluff overlooking the Kentucky River. An abandoned railroad bridge sat in the near distance, awaiting conversion to a bungee-jumping platform. The river was 200 feet below me, the equivalent of 20 stories down a steep, verdant hill. And I was sipping bourbon whiskey at the newly inaugurated visitor's center at the Wild Turkey Distillery in Lawrenceburg, Kentucky.

Earlier that day, I toured the distillery. I had passed massive grain silos to start the tour in the fermentation room, which was filled with gigantic vats of bubbling liquid that smelled very much like yeasty corn porridge. I stepped briefly into the blisteringly hot, jungle-humid stillroom before retreating into an air-conditioned hallway. I saw a room larger than a gymnasium, filled with brand new, charred-oak barrels, waiting to be filled. Then I donned a hairnet (and a beard-net) and stepped into the bottling plant, high-tech and brand new, with bottles on conveyers getting filled, labeled, capped, and sealed.

That evening, while savoring the finished product and gazing down at the river, I marveled at the processes—some scientific, some artful—by which simple grains such as corn (or maize), barley, rye, and wheat become whiskey. Mostly, though, I appreciated my good fortune: a beautiful view, a lovely drink, and a day full of bourbon whiskey.

✖✖

Whiskey, to me, is a spirit with a story. The story starts with a humble grain, such as corn or barley. Using techniques both ancient and modern, distillers manipulate the grain to get to its sugar content. Yeasts eat the sugar and excrete alcohol. The process happens in giant fermentation tanks. This liquid, which tastes somewhat like an unhopped beer, then gets pumped into stills, where it undergoes a round or three of distillation, becoming unaged whiskey. This liquid goes into barrels, which are then stored in warehouses. The flavor of the resulting whiskey depends on a lot of factors: What kind of wood the barrel is made from, and how that wood was charred, toasted, or otherwise manipulated before the liquid splashed in. Warehouse location plays a role, too: Whiskey on upper levels ages faster than lower-level whiskeys. Climate? Sure. Scotch ages more slowly than does bourbon, for example, which is why you see many 20-year-old Scotches on the market, but few bourbons of that age. The Kentucky climate murders bourbon at about the time when it would be old enough to vote.

Sometimes you can smell the story in the glass. Certain Scotches smell of sea air or heathery meadows of the Lowlands. Sometimes you can taste a winey sweetness from the reused sherry casks a particular Scotch might have aged in. Bourbon smells of the vanilla and caramel compounds it picks up from charred-oak barrels. Rye smells similar, but with a spicier character that might remind you of pulpy, hard-boiled detective novels.

Whiskey cocktails also tell a story. Cherry Bounce comes straight from Martha Washington's recipe diaries and tells tales of revolution and nascent nations. The Manhattan has its origins in an exclusive social club on Fifth Avenue; the Prince of Wales similarly calls to mind wealth and comfort. The Rob Roy speaks of swashbuckling adventure. The Algonquin calls to mind Dorothy Parker; the Cablegram speaks of an era before world wars and cold wars. The Old Pal and the Paddy are avuncular and comforting. The Preakness, the Ward Eight, the Godfather, and the Monte Carlo—those drinks know whom not to double-cross.

WHISKEY, WHISKY, WHATSKY?

Now, there's one thing I'm obligated to get out of the way, and that's how to spell this word, *whiskey*.

When I think about the world my children might inherit, I have many dreams for them—ways in which I want the world to be a better place as they begin careers and start families of their own. I hope my daughter doesn't face a career defined by gender-based income inequality, for example. I hope they never have to stock their homes with DIY flat-pack furniture purchased from primary-colored big-box stores with products named for North Sea fishing villages. And I fervently wish that my kids never have to explain to *anyone* why in the hell the word *whiskey* has two different spellings.

Truth is, no one really knows why *whiskey* has two spellings. Many people have come up with cutesy explanations, but the simplest is this: Just as British

English and American English have variant spellings for such pairs as color/colour and aluminum/aluminium, American and British English also spell *whiskey/whisky* differently. The Irish follow the American model and use the *e*. The Canadians and Japanese follow the British model and leave it out.

Strangely, it wasn't always thus. Go back a hundred years, and you can find references in Scottish publications to "Scotch whiskey." Bottles in Canada surface from time to time showing that Canadian brands like J. P. Wiser's once labeled their bottles with the word *"whiskey."* In the United States, the brand Maker's Mark styles itself "whisky," as do George Dickel Tennessee and Old Forester bourbon. Aaaaargh. As you can see, there are no hard pronouncements to make here.

I must, however, clear up one point of confusion. You sometimes hear people say that whisky and whiskey have different names because they're different things; the claim here is that whisky and whiskey are fundamentally different products (and usually that one type of whiskey is better than all the rest). This is nonsense. Scotch, Canadian, Irish, bourbon, rye, Japanese, craft, whatever—they're all products made from grain, yeast, and water, with added flavors derived from aging in wooden barrels. What differences there are between them are too minor for anyone to claim they're fundamentally different categories of liquor. You might as well assert that BMWs should be named *automobeels* just because they're not an American or Japanese make.

In this book, I will hew to the convention that the American and Irish spelling is whiskey, and that Scotch, Canadian, and Japanese is whisky. When I speak in general terms, I'll use the spelling *whiskey* because I'm an American author writing for an American publisher. Incidentally, the plural of *whiskey* is *whiskeys,* and the plural of *whisky* is *whiskies,* and I'll use each form where it's appropriate.

In the end, all of this is tedious, and I wish the world's whiskey producers would all take the same side, whether that's *whisky* or *whiskey.* Because in the end, the only thing that matters is the drink itself. As the satirical Twitter account Fake AP Stylebook (@FakeAPStylebook) once quipped, "You don't spell whisky, you savor it."

—— *Chapter 1*——

WHAT IS WHISKEY?

Picture the boilermaker. Not a Purdue University student, but the drink order at your local favorite dive bar—a pint of beer and a shot of whiskey. It's nothing fancy, but in some ways there's nothing better. I've had fancy cocktails on hotel rooftops; I've had sophisticated tipples all over the country; and I've tried a decades-old Scotch at one of the best-regarded restaurants in Manhattan, but I'm never too fancy to drink a boilermaker.

Beer and whiskey have a natural affinity for each other, and why is that? Let's look closer at them both to see what they have in common. Beer starts with a grain—malted barley or malted wheat—which is mixed with hot water and left to sit a while. Then yeast is added to ferment the grain-water mixture. Malted barley, yeast, and water—fermented to make an alcoholic beverage. Hell, all you have to do is distill that and you have malt whiskey.

At its essence, then, whiskey is distilled beer—or at least a distillation of beer's cousin—and aged in oak barrels for color, texture, and flavor. No wonder they go so well together, and no wonder, too, that several beer makers today are aging their products in reused bourbon barrels.

Whiskey—no matter its base grain or country of origin—is a liquor distilled from a fermented mash of grain, and then aged for some time in wooden containers. (Corn whiskey—the type that isn't bourbon—is an exception to this rule, but more on that later.) The mash can be a single grain, such as wheat or rye, but it's nearly always a blend of grains. Barley, corn (maize), rye, and wheat are the most frequently used grains, but by law you can take any grain and make it into whiskey. This is why you can now find whiskeys made from quinoa, blue corn, and triticale. Laos, Thailand, and Vietnam all have a tradition of making whiskey from rice. Inspired by that example, a Louisiana distillery called Atelier Vie has released a whiskey made entirely of Louisiana rice.

The crucial point to emphasize, though, is this: modern commercial whiskey is made only of grain—not of fruit or sugar or molasses or vegetables or any other plant matter.

No matter where it's from or what it's made from, all whiskey is essentially the same: a liquor distilled from a fermented mash of grain. And though it doesn't need to be aged to be considered whiskey, in practice nearly all of it sees time in wooden containers. Moreover, all whiskey is essentially made in the same way, too. First, take some grain and then either mill it or grind it. Take the ground-up grain and make a "porridge" with water and yeast. Let that naturally ferment in large tanks. Take the fermented liquid and pump it into a still. Distill it at least twice. Put it into a barrel to age for a while. Cut it with water and bottle it.

One additional commonality among most of the various styles of whiskey is this: they didn't start life as commercial products. Early whiskey was very little like anything we'd recognize today. First, it wasn't always grain based, and it wasn't aged—it was enjoyed straight off the still. It was often unpalatable on its own and so was doctored up with cinnamon and other herbs, honey, and sometimes oatmeal. Distillation was also very much a cottage industry, and the drink was made from surplus grains, fruit, vegetables, and other plant matter that would otherwise go to rot.

The advantages of making whiskey from surplus grain were compelling. They had to be compelling because early stills were dangerous and hard to use. A large tub of flammable liquid atop open flames? What could go wrong? If you're going to risk your life, you need a good reason.

The dangers were worth the effort, though, because spirits can be stored nearly indefinitely (unlike grain, which eventually rots). And when whiskey did become commercial, it fetched more at market than raw grain did, so there was a financial incentive. And perhaps most important, spirits were easier to transport than grain. A horse can pull about four bushels of raw grain in a cart, but in the same cart it can pull 60 barrels of whiskey, the equivalent of 24 bushels of grain. Geography also imposed constraints on shipping grain.

As farm products, Irish, Scotch, bourbon, rye, and Canadian whiskeys all developed in the same way. The other major category of whiskey, Japanese, on the other hand, started as a deliberate industry, modeled on the Scotch industry.

This chapter necessarily glosses over a lot of important differences between

whiskey categories. I will nonetheless explain key aspects of those differences. If you're new to whiskey, and you have no idea what separates a Scotch whiskey from an Irish, or a Canadian from a bourbon, the simple truth is there's not as much a difference as you might think. Think of the world's great whiskeys as cousins on a family tree. For all their differences, they're very much related. And once you understand the subtleties of one whiskey, you can learn the nuances of them all.

THE WHISKEY FIVE

All whiskeys belong in one of five categories. First, you have **malt whiskey.** It's the oldest style around, and it might be the most revered. Malt whiskey is made purely of barley malt, also known as malted barley. I'll cover the malting process later. It's made in pot stills and it's generally aged in used barrels. Single malt Scotch falls in this category, but so do whiskeys from the United States, Japan, Ireland, and other countries. Malt whiskeys are good in certain kinds of cocktails, though their subtleties can get lost in other kinds of cocktails. I'll talk about when it's appropriate to use them in mixed drinks.

Next up is **grain whiskey.** It's made in column stills, mostly from raw grain (that is, grain that isn't malted). Most grain whiskey is used in blends. It's the backbone of most blends, in fact, providing smoothness and light flavor. A few grain whiskeys are available for purchase. They're usually light and floral and good for sipping, but they're not always good for cocktails, where they get lost in the mix. Because of this, I won't talk much about grain whiskey in this book.

The largest-selling category of whiskey in the world is **blended whiskey.** It is made in most of the world from rich malt or straight whiskeys and one or more aged grain whiskeys. American blends typically cut straight whiskey with something so close to vodka that the flavor is stripped out. These are bottom-shelf rotgut, and they are not at all good for much of anything. The best blends are from Canada, Scotland, Ireland, and Japan. They're generally good for cocktails, and I have quite a few recipes that call for them.

Irish single pot still whiskey is made in a pot still from both malted and unmalted barley. It's rich and smooth, delicious to drink on its own. Because it's so good on its own, I don't mix it into cocktails often. But I do have a couple of recipes that sing for it—and that will make you sing when you taste them.

Straight whiskey rounds out this list. Here you have bourbon and rye. *Straight* simply means an unblended American whiskey, made in column stills and aged at least two years in new oak containers. Straight whiskey is wonderful sipped on its own, but it also works very well in cocktails.

So don't be intimidated. Whiskey is a complicated topic, but at its heart it's only grain, water, yeast, and wood. Nothing complicated about that.

Because these four ingredients are at the heart of what makes whiskey whiskey, and because every form of whiskey on the planet requires all four of them, I'm going to take some time to discuss these four ingredients and talk about how each type of whiskey uses them. In this way, I hope to give you an understanding of how all whiskeys are fundamentally the same, even as they possess unique elements that define their style.

GRAIN

All whiskey starts with cereal grains, the seeds of a tall grass cultivated for staple crops. Whole grains are a great source of nutrition—vitamins, minerals, fats and oils, proteins, and carbohydrates. This last—carbohydrate—is what whiskey makers are primarily looking for in the fermentation process. Namely, what they're looking for is the starch locked in the endosperm.

Starch, however, isn't easily fermentable. When yeast is hungry, it's not looking for starch but rather a lower-hanging fruit: sugar. The first step in making whiskey is to get at the sugars that are locked inside the grain. You need to get to those so that they can ferment into alcohol. Different whiskey regions do this in different ways.

The solution that Scotch producers use is to malt the grain. The grain, in this case, is barley. To malt barley, producers steep it in water for up to two days, drain the water off, spread the grain out on a flat surface, and allow the grain to sprout. The sprouting process starts an enzymatic reaction inside the barley grain that breaks down the proteins that lock the starches in place inside the grain. As the grain sprouts, the shoot eats the starches and converts them to sugars. When the barley reaches a sweet spot where most of the starches have been consumed but the grain hasn't fully eaten itself, the germination process is stopped by heating the barley in a kiln.

——•• WHAT IS PEAT? ••——

Peat is partially decomposed vegetable matter found in mires or bogs. If peat is allowed to just do its thing, after thousands of years it eventually becomes coal. Peat most commonly consists of sphagnum moss, and it's been an important fuel source around the world for thousands of years. Peat for fuel is compressed and dried out so that it will burn.

Scotland is rich in peat and, historically, burning peat was the most cost-effective way to produce barley malt because it was the cheapest fuel for fire. Peat was also the main fuel for heating pot stills, though that process did little to contribute smoky flavors to the whisky.

Peat habitats cover over 20 percent of Scotland's landmass, and though peatlands are in no current danger of depletion, the whisky industry and the Scottish government are nevertheless taking steps to conserve this natural resource. Distilleries have adopted a variety of techniques to burn peat more efficiently, and the government has mounted an effort to manage and restore the country's peatlands.

Scotland doesn't produce the world's only peated whiskies, though. Irish producers use homeland peat for smoking barley, and several American microdistillers use peat harvested in Canada and the United States, also for the purpose of smoking barley.

For whiskeys that are *peated*, this is when the peat is introduced in the process. In most kilns, only hot air is used to dry and heat the barley, and that hot air doesn't introduce any additional flavors to the barley. Historically, though, Scotch producers would burn peat to produce a smoke that would heat and dry the barley. This peat smoke lent a distinctive smoky note to the finished product. Peat was once an economic necessity for Scotch production because it was the cheapest fuel for malting the barley. Today, however, it's an optional element that some producers use to give their Scotch a distinctive taste and aroma.

Corn is another story; it doesn't take well to malting. Distillers need to break down the starches in corn to get the enzyme reactions. The corn is milled and cooked and then blended with a little bit of barley malt, which provides the enzymes that are needed to attack the starch.

Rye can be malted like barley, or it can go into a mash unmalted; it depends on the preferences of the distiller and the flavor profile he or she is looking for. Some use malted, some use unmalted, and others use a combination.

—•◦ THE BIG FOUR ◦•—

A vast array of grains can go into whiskey: corn (maize), barley, rye, wheat, triticale (a wheat-rye hybrid), quinoa, rice, millet, buckwheat, oats, and so on. But whiskey has its Big Four, the grains that are found either alone or in some combination in nearly all the world's whiskeys: barley, corn, rye, and wheat.

Either barley or corn is most often used for the base, with wheat and rye usually acting as flavoring grains. Scotland, Ireland, and Japan favor barley, whereas North America favors corn. Bourbon uses a mix of mostly corn, with rye or wheat adding additional flavor, and a little malted barley to help starches break down. Canadian whisky starts with corn as the base grain, and almost exclusively uses rye as the flavoring grain. (Only one Canadian distillery today uses wheat as the flavoring grain.) In both Canada and the United States, you can find some all-rye whiskeys, but they're the exception.

Wheat and rye round out the Big Four. In most whiskeys, these are flavoring grains, there to complement the main grain. Wheat is soft-tasting and enhances the sweetness of corn. Rye is spicy and earthy and brings a robust flavor to the whiskeys it flavors.

WATER

Spend any amount of time reading about Scotch whisky, and it won't take long for you to encounter flowery prose about volcanic eruptions giving birth to the Scottish highlands, glaciers forming the glens (or valleys) of the region, the icy waters of rivers coursing through those glens, and the springs bubbling from the dark earth.

Bourbon is no different, except that bourbon writers emphasize the limestone through which rainfall trickles, filtering out iron deposits in the water that can make bourbon taste rusty if you fail to get rid of them. As you drive around central Kentucky, making your way from the Maker's Mark distillery to the Woodford Reserve plant, you pass horse farms, long white fences, and fields full of Kentucky's famed bluegrass. Images of Bourbon Country show horses galloping through verdant meadows, making you wonder whether horses and hooch have anything in common other than a state of origin. Yes, in fact, they do. The very limestone through which bourbon's water supply trickles also provides calcium to the grass, which horses then use to build stronger bones, thus making them faster, better racers.

WATER'S ROLE IN MASHING

Water plays an important role in the mashing process, which is when milled grain is mixed with water and cooked to the proper temperature for fermentation. In Kentucky, bourbon makers look for limestone-filtered water with plenty of calcium and absolutely no iron. Calcium helps feed the yeast in the fermentation process, controls pH levels, and encourages the development of certain congeners (flavor-making chemicals in the finished whiskey). Contrast this to iron that turns bourbon black and rusty-tasting. Scotch makers, however, are looking for a softer water, with minerals that help promote yeasts during fermentation.

The mash at this point resembles a thick porridge or oatmeal. Because the goal is to convert starches into fermentable sugars, the temperature needs to be just right. If it's too cold, nothing will happen at all; but if it's too hot, the enzymes that break down the starches will disintegrate.

YEAST

After the mash sits long enough to convert the starch to sugar, it gets pumped into fermentation tanks, where yeast is added. Yeast is a unicellular organism in the fungus kingdom. Yeast eats saccharified grains—that is, a process in which the starches have turned to sugars—and produces alcohol, carbon dioxide, water, and various other compounds that contribute to the flavors and aromas of whiskey, such as esters and ketones.

Most large whiskey makers produce their own yeast in on-site labs, nurturing cultures that have survived for as many as fifty years or more. Chris Morris, master distiller at Woodford Reserve, describes the process as follows: His technicians go into the lab and take a pinprick of yeast from a culture growing there. That pinprick goes into a small flask of malt syrup, where it grows and grows until it is ready to be placed into a larger flask. And on the process goes until, by the end of one week, Woodford has 600 gallons of yeast grown from that pinprick.

The differences between yeasts is immediately noticeable when you have a chance to tour distilleries and see (and smell) the fermentation rooms. Every distillery's tanks smell like yeast and porridge, but beyond those obvious aromas, you can detect scents individual to each distillery.

Wild Turkey's tanks, for example, smell like baked apple, cinnamon, and oatmeal, whereas the tanks at Maker's Mark smell like banana bread; Woodford Reserve's tanks remind me of black pepper, red wine, and butter in the younger tanks, and applesauce and pineapple in the older tanks. In each case, the yeast was prompting the growth of certain enzymes in the fermentation process that promoted unique flavors and aromas. As the fermentation process goes on, though, those scents fade to the background, and the mash starts to smell more like beer.

The carbon dioxide then escapes into the air, and the distillation process separates the alcohol from the water. Standing over a fermentation tank, you can smell the CO_2 as it escapes the tank. As Wild Turkey's master distiller, Eddie Russell, says, "A good whiff will clear your sinuses."

Scotch producers use two kinds of yeast: brewer's yeast and baker's yeast. Bourbon makers cultivate their own yeasts (which produce esters that add fruity, floral, round, herbal, or spicy qualities) and keep the strain alive for generation after generation after generation to help ensure the yeast is making a consistent ferment from batch to batch. Cultivating yeast is a skill unto itself—one passed down from generation to generation of whiskey makers. When you think of people deliberately cultivating microorganisms, you might think of hipper-than-thou artisans making sourdough or sauerkraut to sell at farmer's markets to people pushing children in $750 strollers. In bourbon's history, however, it was absolutely necessary to cultivate your own. Back in, say, Jim Beam's day, cultivating it yourself was the only way to go. The Beam family has stories of Jim going out on to his porch to capture wild yeast from the air.

Some distilleries take great pains to use closed fermentation vats or other techniques to keep wild yeast from getting into the fermenting tanks; others don't.

To get an idea of the role of yeast in promoting flavor, consider the Four Roses bourbon distillery, located in Lawrence-burg, Kentucky. Four Roses uses five yeast strains and two mash bills (the proportion of grains in the mix) to create ten distinct whiskeys, which are blended after aging to help Four Roses maintain a consistent product from batch to batch.

None of this is to say there's no role for commercial yeast. Some small distilleries lacking the expertise or resources to culti-vate wild yeast use it. The high-proof grain whiskies that comprise the lion's share of blended Scotch and many Canadian whis-kies start with commercial yeast, too; these grain whiskies are added to the blend to provide bulk rather than flavor. Even single malt Scotch makers use commercial yeast.

DISTILLATION

At its heart, distillation is easy. Alcohol boils at a lower temperature than water does, so to distill wine or beer into liquor, all you need to do is boil it, collect the alcohol vapors as they rise, and cool them down until they condense back into liquid alcohol.

Today's pot stills work very much like they have for centuries. Start with a heat source. Traditionally, that would have been a wood fire. Place a pot filled with wine or beer or cider over the fire. Atop the pot, place a cap to collect the alcohol vapors. This cap ends in what's called a swan's neck, because of its shape. The swan's neck leads to a lyne arm, or a pipe that carries the vapors to a con-denser. The condenser consists of a coiled metal tube inside a metal or wooden chamber.

Start the fire and heat the liquid inside the pot. As the liquid reaches 172°F (78°C), the alcohol starts to boil and vaporize. The vapors rise up into the cap and then into the swan's neck. They move through the lyne arm into a coiled metal tube that is submerged in a condenser chamber filled with cold water. The water chills the vapor in the coiled tube, condensing the vapor back into liquid alcohol.

The resulting alcohol is called *low wines* and is about 25 to 35 percent alcohol by volume. These low wines are distilled again, producing a spirit that's about 70 percent alcohol by volume.

Today, some Irish whiskey and all malt whiskey is produced using pot stills, but modern pot stills are no longer heated by a wood fire. The stills are heated either with gas or electric heat, or with steam.

Pot stills have certain advantages: they produce a deep, rich distillate with a creamy texture. The smooth malty flavors you find in single malts and certain Irish whiskeys have their start in the pot still. The biggest disadvantage, though, is that pot stills need to be emptied and cleaned after each batch. And if you can only achieve a maximum of about 70 percent alcohol by volume in a pot still, it means that you're leaving some alcohol behind in the beer or wine or cider you started with.

For these reasons and more, distillers started tinkering around with continuous distillation in column stills. During the Industrial Revolution of the early 1800s, the column still first arose. But it was an Irishman, Aeneas Coffey, in 1830, who improved upon it and created a design that has lasted, with a few tweaks, to this day.

Grain whiskey makers use a version of the Coffey still that consists of two large copper columns—the analyzer and the rectifier—seated side by side and linked by a pipe at the top. Each column has a series of perforated plates that divide it into chambers. The fermented liquid (or wash) enters the top of the first column, the analyzer, where it meets a jet of steam pumped into the bottom of the analyzer column. As the wash descends, the alcohol within it vaporizes and rises up to meet the perforated plates. Some of the alcohol vapors pass through the perforations, while others meet the plates and condense. This process continues from chamber to chamber, each chamber acting like a mini-still, with distillation occurring hundreds of times in the column as liquid falls and vapor rises.

Eventually, the vaporized alcohol is pumped into the base of the rectifier column, where it begins the process again. The alcohol-laden steam rises through the chambers, but this time each mini-distillation purifies the alcohol, stripping out the heavier higher and lower alcohols, leaving the hearts (the spirit the distiller retains and uses to make beverage alcohol) to rise to the top, where they're pumped off and allowed to condense into nearly pure grain alcohol. This process is much faster and more efficient than pot stills, and even the earliest models of Coffey stills could produce thousands of gallons of alcohol in a few hours.

A double-column Coffey still can produce a distillate that's up to 180 proof, or 90 percent alcohol by volume. Because grain whiskey is used mostly as filler in blends, this high percentage is okay.

Bourbon and rye are also made in column stills, though the still is a one-column setup, not the grain whiskey double column version I just described. Bourbon and rye also then go through what's called a *doubler,* which is basically just a pot still that's used to put finishing touches on the bourbon. (What these touches are is hard to define; different distilleries use them for different reasons.) By law, bourbon and rye cannot be distilled above 160 proof, or 80 percent alcohol by volume. During a tour of the Wild Turkey distillery, master distiller Eddie Russell told our tour group that he pulls Turkey off the still at 128 to 130 proof. "We're cookin' it medium-rare," he explained.

Some distillers also use something called a *hybrid still,* which looks something like a pot still with a column on top of it.

WOOD

You might think it's weird to describe wood as a whiskey ingredient. After all, there's no actual wood in your whiskey. Or is there? Not directly, but many of the molecules and chemicals in the wood certainly end up in your whiskey. The easiest demonstration of this is in the color of the booze; that's the wood at work. And, in some cases, caramel coloring is added.

After the clear spirit comes off the still, it goes into barrels for aging. Most American whiskeys, including all bourbons and ryes, are aged in new oak barrels. By contrast, most Scotch, Canadian, Japanese, and Irish whiskeys are aged in used oak barrels. New oak imparts strong notes of vanilla aromas and flavors; bourbon makers are looking for these vanilla notes, whereas, say, Scotch makers are trying to avoid them.

The use of new oak, incidentally, is the law for both bourbon and rye. By law, straight bourbon and rye *must* be aged in new oak containers. (However, it's also an aspect of whiskey production that American producers tout because it produces a unique style that's popular—and profitable—around the world.) The reason American whiskey uses new oak is lobbying. Barrel makers (coopers) and foresters lobbied Congress to support this law because it protected jobs in their respective industries.

Barrel making is an ancient technology, dating back thousands of years. Winemakers and distillers have known for a long time that a barrel can improve the flavor of liquids stored within it; the French have known for 500 years that charred barrels give flavor and color to brandy. Only within the last few decades, however, has cooperage become a full-on science, with barrel makers studying all the many variables in a barrel that affect flavor.

COOPERAGE—THE ART AND SCIENCE OF BARREL MAKING

In his book *Bourbon, Strange,* the whiskey writer Charles Cowdery explains that up until the middle of the 20th century, the largest users of barrels were the petroleum and beer industries. Their purchasing power meant that all barrels produced in the

United States conformed to their specifications—which obviously didn't have the needs of whiskey makers in mind.

Even decades after those two industries switched to metal containers, coopers continued making barrels in the accustomed way, and didn't start customizing barrels for the needs of the wine and spirits industries until relatively recently. Previously, the only variable that coopers ever changed was the level of char on the interior of the barrel.

Today, however, cooperage is as much a cutting-edge science as it is a venerable technology.

—•► HOW TO MAKE A BARREL ◄•—

Whiskey cooperage, at least in the United States, starts in a stand of American white oak trees, commonly found all over the eastern part of the country. A forester cuts a tree down and typically leaves the logs in the woods to season in the open air for days or even weeks.

The main cooperage for American whiskey is the Independent Stave Company, with locations in Missouri and Kentucky. The company sells barrels to nearly every major—and many minor—whiskey brands in the United States: Wild Turkey, Jim Beam, Four Roses, Evan Williams, Rittenhouse Rye, and Bulleit, among many others.

Aside from Independent Stave, the other major cooperage in the United States is Brown-Forman's, with locations in Kentucky and Alabama. Brown-Forman formerly sold barrels to other companies, but the demand for its alcohol products is now so great that Brown-Forman can

supply barrels for only its own brands now. You might not know the name Brown-Forman, but you surely know its largest brand: Jack Daniel's.

Brown-Forman's Louisville cooperage puts together about 2,500 barrels a day, and I had a chance to watch the process. The company buys wood from lumber mills that cut the wood to its specifications. Brown-Forman hauls the wood to its two cooperages, where it sits out in the yard to air-dry, open to the elements. After months of air-drying, it's then kiln-dried. These drying processes help tame the tannins in the wood; without aging, an oak barrel would produce a tannic, bitter flavor. The staves are then machined into shapes that will fit well together to form a barrel.

Working with remarkable speed, a barrel maker takes the long barrel staves and assembles them into a circle, holding them in place with iron hoops. The assembled barrel is toasted with radiant heat, using a proprietary process.

Toasting the wood breaks its cellulose into wood sugars, which are caramelized in part during the toasting phase, and then in part later, when the barrels are charred. These wood sugars add notes of caramel, which seems obvious, but they also add body to the whiskey. Additionally, toasting converts the wood's lignin into vanillin, which introduces notes of vanilla and cocoa into the whiskey.

After toasting, the barrels are charred with flame. This is a fascinating process to watch. A conveyor moves a group of open-ended barrels over natural gas burners. The burners sense when the barrels are above them and flame to life, catching the barrels' interiors on fire. The flame burns for a few minutes, and then a sprinkler system mists water into the barrels to douse the flames.

Charring turns the innermost layers of the barrel into charcoal. During the aging process, whiskey filters back and forth through the charcoal, which mellows the spirit by stripping out some of the tannins and other compounds that cause bitter or strong flavors. Sherry and other wine barrels are generally not charred, only toasted.

The Brown-Forman Cooperage produces 700 to 800 barrels a day in its Alabama facility, all of which goes to Jack Daniel's. In Louisville, the facility makes 2,400 to 2,500 a day, about 90 percent of which go to Jack.

Today, coopers understand far more about the physical, chemical, and biological properties of oak. The Buffalo Trace Distillery, for example, has an innovative set of experiments going on right now called the Single Oak Project. They're looking at such variables as the size of grain in the wood, whether the wood staves of a barrel originate from the top or bottom of a tree, the length of time in which the staves were left to air-dry, and the char level.

Brown-Forman (makers of Jack Daniel's, Woodford Reserve, and Old Forester, among other brands) has developed proprietary processes for toasting the interior a barrel, and though they won't give specifics, their spokespersons hint that the toasting process varies somewhat for each brand.

Bourbon makers extoll the virtues of new oak barrels, which reasonably enough contribute far more wood flavors to whiskey than do used barrels. Compare a bourbon and a single malt Scotch and you'll see, smell, and taste the difference. The bourbon will be darker in color and have more robust flavors and aromas, whereas the Scotch will be lighter, smoother, and more delicate.

Other than the United States, most of the rest of the world's whiskeys are aged in used whiskey barrels. The source of most of these used barrels is the American whiskey industry. Because bourbon and rye must age in new casks, the American whiskey industry has a lot of extra casks around after their product is bottled for market. The vast majority of these go to the Scotch industry, though many of them go to Ireland, Canada, and Japan as well.

Whiskey makers all over the world—American, Scottish, Irish, Japanese, and Canadian—may also use other types of used barrels in their processes. Used sherry, port, or wine barrels add a fruity nuttiness to the whiskey. Barrels such as these are referred to as *finishing barrels*. You'll find these barrels most commonly used in

Scotch production, but even bourbon makers can use them *after* aging in new oak, as long as the label notes they were used as finishing barrels.

Incidentally, I'm barely scratching the surface of barrel science. Cooperage (the craft of barrel making) is increasingly becoming a science involving chemistry, physics, and the biochemistry of wood. Distillers are excited about this science because it opens up new ways to manipulate and develop the flavors of whiskey. This also enables them to introduce new products to the market. A great example of this is Maker's 46, a product extension of the Maker's Mark line. Maker's 46 arose from the study of cooperage by scientists at Independent Stave, the company that supplies Maker's Mark with its barrels. Independent Stave was working with winemakers to help them age their products by putting seared oak staves into the barrel in an effort to add more oak surface area for the wine to interact with. After many attempts, Independent Stave hit on the right combination of wood varieties and levels of char. To make Maker's 46, the team at Maker's Mark take finished, aged bourbon and age it an extra ten weeks in specially modified barrels that hold French oak staves.

AGING

More factors than just the barrel affect the way whiskey ages—the design and location of the warehouse, for example. Some warehouses are open to the air, whereas some are closed. Some are heated in the winter; others are not. Heating a warehouse somewhat evens out seasonal temperature variations, thus changing the length of time the whiskey needs to age.

Some warehouses are on the tops of hills; some are in valleys. Variations in microclimate affect whiskey aging. Even variations within the warehouse itself affect the way whiskey ages; whiskey on the top floor ages faster than whiskey on the bottom floor.

Oxidation and evaporation also play a role. Oxygen moves in and out of a barrel as the whiskey moves in and out of the wood staves. Meanwhile, both the alcohol and the water in the whiskey evaporates through the wood into the outside air. This concentrates the congeners in the whiskey, including some that the whiskey picks up from the barrel itself. You can smell this evaporation as you enter a whiskey warehouse; the aroma of whiskey is all around you, giving off smells of vanilla and cocoa, warm spices and honey. I've seen many people walk into a whiskey warehouse and breathe deeply, hold their breath, and exhale with a satisfied sigh.

AGE STATEMENTS

Look carefully at a few bottles of whiskey the next time you're shopping. Look for a number telling you how old the whiskey is. It's usually listed as an age, if it's on there at all. So, for example, the bottle might tell you the whiskey is 12 years old. Sometimes, though, it's expressed as a year, letting you know the whiskey was distilled in, say, 1995. If a bottle carries an age statement, that age statement refers to the *youngest* whiskey in the bottle. So if it's 12 years old, all of the whiskey is at least 12 years old; some of it might be older, though in practice, little of it will be.

BLENDING AND BATCHING WHISKEY

Having established that whiskey is grains, water, yeast, and wood, I need to point out a fact about blended whiskey that many whiskey drinkers don't know: Nearly every whiskey you drink is blended. Scotch, Irish, Canadian, bourbon, rye, Tennessee, Japanese, you name it. It's almost all blended.

"Wait, Dietsch," you might ask, "what about single malt?" Yep, blended.

Now, I should clarify what that means. There's an informal way to use the word *blend* and a formal way. Informally, a blend is a mixture of whiskeys from two or more barrels (which barrels are blended is determined by the brand's master distiller). In Scotland, however, *blended Scotch* is a specific legal designation, defining it as a blend of one or more single malts with grain whisky. (I'll talk more about single malt Scotch, grain whisky, and blended Scotch in Chapter 2.) This can be confusing, using one word to mean two things. So moving forward, I'll use *blend* in the formal or legal sense, to describe a malt whiskey blended with grain whiskey. And for the informal sense, I'll use the word *batched,* which simply means a mixture of whiskeys from two or more barrels that are married together in a giant vat before being diluted to bottling strength and then bottled.

So to revise my statement above, nearly every whiskey you drink is batched from multiple barrels.

But why do whiskey makers batch in the first place?

Let's say you're the master distiller at the Thomas Lincoln bourbon distillery (I made that up; don't bother calling your retailer demanding Thomas Lincoln). You want to make sure that every bottle of Thomas Lincoln Six Year Old bourbon

"Batching is how you build consistency."

—CHRIS MORRIS,
master distiller at Woodford Reserve

tastes like every previous bottle of Thomas Lincoln Six Year Old bourbon. You know that your customers *also* expect Thomas Lincoln bourbon to taste the same, bottle after bottle and year after year, and yet you also know that many things can affect the flavor of the whiskey in a particular barrel: the quality of the grain used at the beginning; seasonal and yearly weather changes at the aging warehouse (whiskey ages faster in hotter years); the location of the barrel in the warehouse (barrels in upper floors are hotter—heat rises, remember—and therefore age more quickly than barrels in lower levels); and how the wood for the barrel is selected, aged, charred, and shaped into barrels.

To achieve a consistent product from year to year and bottle to bottle, whiskey makers batch barrels together to produce a whiskey with all the characteristics consumers expect from a certain brand. If the whiskey in a certain barrel is spicier than the brand's aficionados would expect, the blender uses a milder barrel to balance that out. If the barrel has imparted too much woody flavor into the whiskey, it will be married to whiskey from a less woody barrel.

If a bottle carries an age statement—for example, our hypothetical Thomas Lincoln Six Year Old—every barrel that gets mixed into the final product needs to have aged at least the amount of time the age statement declares. So, to look at Mr. Lincoln again, that would mean every barrel in the final batch is at least six years old. Some of the barrels might be 10 or 12 years old, though most of them will be six to eight years old.

All whiskey makers do this. Unless the whiskey you're buying says *Single Barrel* (or *Single Cask,* if Scotch), it's a batched whiskey. Single-barrel whiskeys hold their own delights; they often have nuances you don't find in the flagship bottling. I don't generally suggest them for cocktails, because their unique characteristics are best enjoyed either neat or on the rocks. You might, however, experiment with single-barrel whiskeys in an old-fashioned, where the simplicity of the other ingredients allows the single barrel to shine.

Batching and blending are art forms, and they're practiced differently based on where you are in the world. Bourbon makers batch using barrels of bourbon made at a particular distillery. At Woodford Reserve, for example, master distiller Chris Morris would make a batch of Woodford by sampling barrels in the Woodford distillery and batching together the ones he feels will make a whiskey that matches the Woodford taste profile.

Blended Scotch works a little differently. First, only a few Scottish distilleries make grain whisky, and so most of the grain whisky in the many blended Scotch brands comes from those few distilleries. A company such as Diageo, for example, will buy in bulk enough grain whisky from one of those few distilleries to supply the needs of its blended-whisky brands. Among others, Diageo's brands include Bell's, Buchanan's, J&B, and, most famously, Johnnie Walker.

So if all the grain whiskies in a Diageo blend are from an outside distillery, what about the malt whiskies? Are they exclusively Diageo products? Perhaps; perhaps not. The malts in a given blend are a trade secret, but it's always been common in Scotland for distilleries to trade whiskies with each other for their blends.

Irish and Canadian whiskeys follow a similar model to Scotch, with grain whiskeys added to batches of barley whiskey (in Ireland) or batches of rye whisky (in Canada) to produce the final product. (Canadian whisky has some specific differences, which I'll discuss in more detail later.)

Japanese makers, on the other hand, do things differently still. Scotland has over 100 distilleries making single malt whisky, more than enough to foster an active whisky-bartering culture. Japan has a mere handful, and the big two—Suntory and Nikka—are so fiercely competitive that they'd never trade whiskies. Japanese distillers make a variety of styles of whisky within their own walls: smoky ones, fruity ones, sweet ones, old whiskies, young whiskies, you name it. They then blend together whiskies made within their own walls to form their signature products.

Earlier I mentioned that, in Scotland, *blended Scotch* is a specific legal designation, defining it as a blend of one or more single malts with grain whisky. Now it's time to explain that. Let's start with *single malt*. This is a common term, one you're almost certainly familiar with. What does it mean? First, what does *malt* mean? That's easy; it's just whisky made from malted barley. The hard

part is single, because it doesn't mean what you might think it means. In this case it means not a single barrel or a single batch, but a single distillery. In other words, a single malt is a malt whiskey from one distillery. A single malt could be, and usually is, the result of batching up a number of barrels from that single distillery to achieve the flavor profile that consumers associate with that particular single malt.

Single malt, according to the laws of the United Kingdom, must be a Scotch whisky distilled in one or more batches, *at a single distillery*, from water and malted barley only, and in pot stills. That's pretty simple. Realize, though, that when the law says "one or more batches," that means that single malt can be (and usually is) batched up in the informal sense I detailed earlier. If you buy Glenmorangie 18 Year Old, for example, you'll get a whisky made from malted barley and water, all from the Glenmorangie distillery, made in pot stills. The whisky in your bottle will come from a batch made up of the booze from many barrels, each of which will have held the Scotch for at least 18 years, and some for longer than that.

Let's take it a step further. Blended whisky, by UK law, means a blend of one or more single malts with one or more *single grain whiskies*. Single grain? This word *single* is tricksy, like hobbitses. Single grain doesn't mean it's made from a single grain, like corn or wheat. Oh no! Why would you think that?! It's grain whisky from a single distillery. A grain whisky is a whisky made from barley and other grains, such as wheat and corn. Single-grain whisky can be, and usually is, made in high-volume column stills. The flavor is lighter and less rich than most single malts. Blenders use grain whisky as the main ingredient in most blends, with the single malts added in to provide character, aroma, and flavor. The more expensive the blend, generally speaking, the higher the proportion of single malt.

One more point: Blended Scotch whisky is a blend of many single malts with single-grain whisky, but this doesn't mean that all single malts are from the same distillery. In fact, it's common practice to use single malts from throughout an entire region of Scotland, or sometimes from all of Scotland. The two main drinks giants, Diageo (owner of Johnnie Walker) and Pernod Ricard (owner of Chivas Regal) own many distilleries in Scotland for the purpose of blending the whisky from those distilleries into the mix. Blenders also swap barrels with other producers.

JOHN GLASER

John Glaser is a modern master of the venerable art of blending Scotch whisky. Hailing from the midwestern United States, John lives an expat life with his family in London. There he runs the Compass Box Whisky Company, which offers a line of whisky blends unlike anything else on the market. He pores over 19th-century blended-whisky recipes, buys the best single malts and grain whiskies from whisky makers all over Scotland, takes them back to his blending lab in London, and carefully creates blends that highlight specific flavor profiles.

His Asyla blend is light and fruity. The Peat Monster is, well, a monster of rich, smoky flavors of peat and earth. Oak Cross highlights the flavors imparted by oak barrels. Hedonism is a blend solely made of grain whisky, with its light, round flavors of vanilla.

These whiskies are fantastic, sipped neat or on the rocks, and bartenders enjoy mixing with them, especially The Peat Monster, which lends a nice campfire note to cocktails. They're not really everyday drinks, though, retailing for $50 and up.

But the engine that drives Compass Box now is Glaser's Great King Street editions. Designed to be mixable, Great King Street is also meant for daily drams, selling for around $35 a bottle. Glaser currently has two expressions of Great King Street: the Artist's Blend and the Glasgow Blend. The Artist's Blend is light and mildly fruity, with flavors of vanilla and caramel. Glasgow has hints of smoke, dried fruit, and wine. Both are great in highballs, and in cocktails such as the Morning Glory Fizz (page 118) and the Mamie Taylor (page 149).

──•· WHAT IS MOONSHINE? ·•──

Many people have a misconception about moonshine, which is that it's unaged whiskey, or "white dog," as the bourbon people call it. This is sometimes true—but generally it's not, though "moonshine" producers like to foster that image.

First off, a lot of products have hit shelves over the last few years that call themselves moonshine, and all of those products are lying to you. By definition, moonshine is illegally made liquor. If you see a product on a store shelf, that product is made by a licensed producer in a highly regulated facility, governed by laws passed at the local, state, and federal level. Government pokes its finger into every aspect of liquor making, including the till. In a word: taxation. Illegal liquor on a liquor store shelf? Highly unlikely. I refer to store-bought "moonshine" as *fauxshine*.

Much of the true moonshine—by which I mean illegal hooch—is made from simple table sugar these days. "Sugar shine," as it's known, is fast and cheap to make, and most of it is sold at tremendous profit to so-called nip joints—illicit drinking establishments—across America. You find nip joints in the same towns and neighborhoods where you find men and women addicted to crack and crystal meth. Moonshine, in these communities, is an addictive substance and just as life-wrecking as any other illicit drug. In his 2010 book, *Chasing the White Dog,* author Max Watman describes what the stuff tastes like. He pours a shot, sniffs at it curiously, and then puts his honker deep into the glass as if he were nosing a 1990 Bordeaux. He takes a deep whiff of the sugar shine. The odor hits him so hard he gasps, coughs, and stops to catch his breath. It takes him a full day to work up the courage to taste it. Here's how he describes the experience:

Steeling myself, I took a sip.

Bile. As if I'd burped up vomit. But stomach acid and puke is thick and viscous; this was sharp and thin. As if you took the stomach acid from acid reflux and strained it through a cheesecloth and blended in a dash of simple syrup to sweeten it . . .

There was no lingering flavor. The drink pushed into my mouth, exploded, and then vanished, leaving me feeling as if I'd swirled with some sort of experimental kerosene-powered mouthwash.

I hadn't had anything like a whole shot. Perhaps I'd drunk half an ounce before my right cheek went numb and I poured my glass back into the bottle.

It's the only liquor I've ever had that made me feel that I was hurting myself. I could feel my liver squirm when it hit. I could feel the drip of lead salts depositing themselves into a pocket of my brain.

This was complete shit.

I quote Watman so extensively because so many people cling to a romantic illusion of shine as some sort of frontier whiskey, unaged but made of corn and rye, sipped by mountain men with corncob pipes and beards down to their navels. This image is true to an extent; some illicit distillers take an artisan's approach to their craft, but many—perhaps most—are truly only in it for a buck. And if their product is vile tasting or even dangerous, they don't care. Profit is their only motive.

Historically, the frontier image was true, and moonshine was indeed simply unaged distillate made of corn mash. That is, it was whiskey made without benefit of a wooden barrel.

Some licensed producers today make this type of "moonshine." This practice is especially popular among new distilleries. Making aged whiskey is financially difficult for many start-up distilleries, as it requires the start-up to invest a lot of money in equipment, supplies, and ingredients without seeing any return on that investment for years. So a common business model for young distillers is to sell unaged products—gin, vodka, and "moonshine"—while waiting for their whiskeys to age. Some of these products are new-make (just off the still) whiskey, and though they don't taste like the aged stuff, they have charms of their own. Seek out a small, local distillery, if you happen to live near one. Chances are strong that they'll have an unaged whiskey on hand for you to taste. And if the distillery has an aged whiskey also available, taste them together; you can learn a lot about the base flavors of the distillate from the unaged product, and you'll learn about the influence of wood aging by tasting the aged.

Another branch of "moonshine" that's commercially available is new-make from established distilleries. Some of these products were released to capitalize on the "moonshine" fad of the last few years; others are experimental releases designed to let whiskey aficionados experience the taste and body of new-make versions of established products. For example, I had the chance recently to taste a new-make version of Rittenhouse Rye whiskey. I found that the rye flavor was a lot more present than in the aged version.

But beware, some "moonshine" is a trick, almost a fraud; many products contain grain neutral spirits—vodka, basically—purchased in bulk and bottled in vessels that show race cars or hillbillies or some other Southern cliché. For the price you pay, you could get two (or three!) bottles of plastic-bottle vodka, pour it into Mason jars, and fool your friends into thinking they're drinking something with cachet.

I don't have a problem with new-make whiskey that's sold as such, but I have an aversion to the idea of taking grain neutral spirits and selling that as "moonshine" to young urbanites, especially when the bottle evokes frontier or Appalachian imagery. These producers are engaging in cultural appropriation to sell a lie to gullible fools.

—— Chapter 2 ——

INTRODUCTION TO INTERNATIONAL WHISKEY

Whiskey is truly a worldwide product, having spread from its roots in Gaelic-speaking nations, taking seed in North America, and eventually colonizing the planet. Having discussed the things that are common to all whiskeys (grain, water, yeast, and wood), I'll spend the next few chapters discussing the things that separate Scotch from Irish whiskey, bourbon from Canadian whisky, and so on.

The origins of whiskey are murky. No one knows for certain whether it originated in Ireland or Scotland, for example, or even whether it might have had a whiskey-like ancestor that predated distilling in the British Isles.

A full history of beverage alcohol is well beyond the reaches of this book, but records show alcohol distillation happening in places as geographically distinct as Italy and China, starting in the 12th century. However, the legends that have accrued around Irish whiskey suggest that Irish monks traveling in the Mediterranean in the 10th century brought home the art of distilling alcohol.

As I so often say in this book, no one really knows the full history. What we do know is that the first historical record of whiskey in Ireland comes in 1405; in Scotland, 1494. I'll take history at its word and start the story in Ireland.

IRISH WHISKEY

Irish whiskey was once the belle of the whiskey ball, the most popular spirit in the world. At the height of its whiskey industry, Ireland boasted over 90 distilleries, and at its nadir only two of those remained alive. Today, Irish whiskey still takes a backseat in global markets to Scotch and bourbon, although the category is on an upswing. Irish whiskey is the fastest growing spirits category by sales, and it's immensely popular with young women. The Irish idea of whiskey is a spirit that's rich but smooth, mildly malty, with a hint of fruit and honey. At least five distilleries have opened in Ireland over the last few years, with others on the drafting table. What caused this fine spirit to decline, and what's sparking its modern revival?

A SHORT HISTORY OF IRISH WHISKEY

The origins of Irish whiskey are unclear. I made note earlier of the legend of the peripatetic monks returning home blessed with having learned the secrets to distilling the waters of life. The Latin phrase for "water of life" was aqua vitae, though the Irish preferred their native Gaelic term, *uisge beatha*. (For a rough pronunciation, say "ooskee bay-ha.") Over the years, this term was shortened to *usquebaugh* ("ooskeebah") and, later, *whiskey*.

Irish whiskey initially took off as the by-product of agriculture. Farmers who grew barley had too much to sell, and so they distilled it. (You'll see this story a few more times in this book because Scotch, bourbon, and Canadian all have similar origins.)

By the 17th century, though, the market was ready for commercial distillation. Now-familiar names begin to pop up. Bushmills started in 1608; John Jameson opened his Bow Street Distillery in Dublin in 1780; and James Power opened just a few years later, also in Dublin. By 1901, the Irish whiskey industry was thriving and Irish whiskey was the leading spirit in Great Britain. Irish whiskey enjoyed the support of London exporters, who preferred its mild flavor to Scotch's heavier profile. These exporters shipped Irish whiskey worldwide, providing the industry with a thriving global market.

These golden years didn't last long, though, for the wheels that eventually caused Irish whiskey's downfall were already in motion.

The first blow came from their neighbors across the Irish Sea. Scotch, as a product category, never really took off internationally until the rise of blends. Blended Scotches were designed to be more mellow and smooth than the single malts of the time, and they therefore appealed to a broader audience. As blended Scotch became more competitive to a global audience, Irish whiskey began to slowly lose market share. But Irish whiskey faced two even bigger dangers that nearly destroyed it.

The first arose in 1912—and I mean arose in the sense of an uprising. Seeking an independent Irish republic, demonstrators rebelled against the British Crown (leading eventually to the Irish War of Independence, which lasted from 1919 to 1921). The English punished the Irish upstarts by blockading Irish ports and closing English markets to Irish exports. As I mentioned earlier, it was merchants in London who had been shipping Irish whiskey all around the world. During all this turmoil, these London merchants put a stop to that practice.

At first, Irish distillers weren't entirely worried. After all, they still had the thriving American market, which drank Irish whiskey by the barrel. Who needs London when you can ship directly to New York City? A momentous pair of events in January 1919, however, changed all that.

On January 16, 1919, the United States ratified the Eighteenth Amendment to its Constitution, making Prohibition the law of the land. (It would take a year for Prohibition to finally take effect, but when it did, whiskey sales plummeted.) And just five days later, on January 21, Ireland declared its independence from Great Britain, after centuries of uprisings against the English Crown. Though London merchants were more than happy to ship Scotch whisky to Canada (from whence it was easily smuggled into America), Irish whiskey lacked that advantage, thanks to British trade embargoes against the nascent Irish Republic.

The twin hammers of Prohibition and revolution wounded Irish whiskey so badly that the industry is only still recovering today, nearly a century on.

By the 1980s, closures and consolidations had left the island of Ireland with only four major brands, all owned by one company with a monopoly on the industry. That company put all its marketing weight behind the promotion of Jameson as an international powerhouse brand. And even today, many drinkers think of Jameson when they think Irish whiskey, just as many drinkers think of Jack Daniel's when they think of American whiskey.

Finally, in 1987, a new company rose up to challenge the monopoly when the Cooley Distillery opened on the Cooley Peninsula in County Louth. The distillery wasn't really new; it had made potato-based alcohol previously. But Cooley converted it over to whiskey production. Twenty years later, Cooley reopened the long-shuttered Kilbeggan Distillery. Since then, other distilleries have opened.

The Irish whiskey industry is nowhere near its former glory, but its recovery has been stunning to watch.

IRISH WHISKEY: WHAT IT IS AND HOW TO MAKE IT

Irish whiskey carries a simple legal definition. It must be made in Ireland of cereal grains—malted or unmalted barley, corn, wheat, or so on—and then aged for at least three years, also in Ireland. That makes sense, right? Irish whiskey must be Irish.

Though Irish whiskey can contain any cereal grain, in practice it all starts with barley, much like Scotch. The main difference between the two is that Scotch starts with entirely malted barley, whereas Irish whiskey starts with a mix of malted and unmalted barley.

The distiller dries the barley in a kiln, in most cases without the use of peat smoke (although the Connemara brand is peated). The barley is then ground up and steeped in water to ferment. The fermented liquid is then distilled and aged in new or previously used oak barrels for at least three years. Depending on the brand, some Irish whiskeys are then blended with grain whiskey prior to bottling.

SINGLE MALT IRISH WHISKEY

In the world of Irish whiskey, single malt means the same thing as it does in the world of Scotch: it designates a whiskey made entirely from malted barley and entirely at one single distillery. Brands include Bushmills, Tyrconnell, Knappouge Castle, and Tullamore Dew.

SINGLE POT STILL WHISKEY

The world of whiskey is full of terms that seem to mean one thing and actually mean another. One example is *single grain whiskey,* which means, as I mentioned earlier, a grain whiskey from a single distillery, and not, as you might think, a whiskey made from a single grain. Another example is *single pot still whiskey*. (You'll also see this called *pure pot still whiskey,* but *single* is the legally correct designation.) You'd think that this means any old whiskey made in a pot still. It doesn't. It means whiskey made with a mash bill of both malted and unmalted barley. This is *then* distilled in a pot still, so that part makes sense. But what the definition means is that you can't make single pot still whiskey from entirely malted barley. If there's not some unmalted barley in there as well, then it's not single pot still.

Why does this matter? The blend of malted and unmalted barley produces a whiskey that is unique in character, rich and nutty, smooth and supple. I find these whiskeys to be some of the most sippable examples I've ever tried. Brands to look for include Redbreast and Green Spot. These are fantastic sippers on their own, but are they mixable in cocktails? Read on.

HOW TO MIX WITH IRISH WHISKEY

Irish whiskey is excellent in cocktails, but as with Scotch, you need to distinguish between mixing with blended whiskeys versus mixing with single malts or single pot still whiskeys. Most blended brands are mellow enough to mix well with other ingredients without being overbearing. As you move up the price ladder into single malts and single pot still whiskeys, you can find some singular expressions of the form that rival anything coming out of Scotland.

You can use single malts and single pots in cocktails, but you need to be careful so that you don't lose the subtle flavors of these delicate whiskeys. Though I know some aficionados who say you should never mix with premium Irish whiskey, I find that I love whiskeys such as the aforementioned Redbreast in Irish coffee, where the rich maltiness of the whiskey marries beautifully with the nutty, chocolatey flavors of good, fresh coffee. For drinks with citrus or vermouth, though, I'd use a good blended whiskey because the subtleties of a single-malt Irish whiskey or a single pot still whiskey will get lost in the drink.

I mentioned the peated Connemara earlier. This brand is smoky and richly earthly. If smoky whiskey is your style, you should check it out, even if just to sip. If you want to play with it in cocktails, though, I'd suggest it as a secondary ingredient (alongside another Irish whiskey) to add a layer of smoky flavor. For example, make yourself a Tipperary (page 145), but rinse the glass (see page 91, The Flavor Rinse) with Connemara first.

Now, let us grab a ferry across the Irish Sea and check in with Scotland.

SCOTCH WHISKY

For over a century, Scotch has been the top-selling whisky in the world, and this trend looks likely to continue. Blended Scotch leads the pack. In 2013, exports of Scotch totaled £4.3 billion. Of this, £3.3 billion was blended Scotch. So, though single malts may get the lion's share of media attention, it's blended Scotch that drives the industry. It's blended Scotch that also generally works best in cocktails.

Before we dive into blended Scotch (and, really, who wouldn't want to take a swim in Scotch?), it's important to understand what Scotch itself is, how it became so popular, and where it might be going in the future.

A SHORT HISTORY OF SCOTCH WHISKY

Though the history of Scotch distilling is as murky as a foggy fen, we know that its roots go back to as early as the 15th century. The first record of distilling in Scotland appears in the Exchequer rolls for 1494: "Eight bolls of malt to Friar John Cor, wherewith to make aqua vitae." A boll is 140 pounds, which means eight of them totaled over 1,000 pounds. Clearly, the good Friar Cor managed a large operation, and produced more Scotch than needed for private consumption.

Early Scotch distillation was very much a cottage industry, made from surplus grains that would otherwise go to rot. As whisky production began to be taxed, farmer-distillers went to great lengths to avoid paying those taxes. In the Highlands, most distilling at this time was illicit, conducted in deep glens (valleys) or high up on mountaintops, where auditors for the government couldn't find them.

One unforeseen side effect of the various acts passed for the purpose of taxing spirits is worth mentioning. The Distillery Act of 1786 made a simple error in that it assumed a still could only produce one batch of spirit every 24 hours. This inspired distillers to design new types of stills that could produce spirits faster and more efficiently, eventually leading to the full industrialization of whisky-making.

It was during the 1700s that a certain farm family—the eventual founders of Glenlivet—became established in the Highlands. A man named John Gow moved into the area to escape the English. To further deflect attention, he also changed the Gaelic family name Gow to the more English-sounding Smith. He and his family settled in to farm and distill whisky.

By 1792, when John Smith's grandson George was born, the family had become well established in their new community, farming the Upper Drumin holding in a village called Glenlivet. Andrew, son of John, at his peak was distilling a hogshead a week of illegal whisky. It's hard to know what a hogshead equaled at the time, but in modern terms, it's about 225 to 250 liters, or about 60 to 65 U.S. gallons. Regardless, it's a lot of hooch. When Andrew died in 1817, George took over both farm and distillery, naming both for the village Glenlivet.

By 1795, Scottish merchants were establishing themselves as middlemen. In this year, a man named William Hill set up shop in Edinburgh to sell whisky at his wine store. These merchants were normally wine sellers or grocers who would buy whisky in bulk from distillers, and often blend it in-store to ensure consistency before selling it to customers. Several major brands of blended Scotch started out this way, including Johnnie Walker, Chivas Regal, and Dewar's.

Illicit distilling and smuggling continued to be a huge concern in Scotland, with even Members of Parliament known to trade in the very contraband their own august body had made illegal. It wasn't long before Parliament realized it needed to provide a legal path for illicit distillers to turn legitimate. The result was the 1823 Act to Eliminate Illicit Distilling.

In a span of 11 years (1823–1834), the number of seized illicit stills dropped from 1,400 to 692. New licensed distilleries arose in the decades just after the Act of 1823, including several brands still familiar to us today: Talisker in 1830; Glen Scotia in 1832; Glenfarclas in 1836; Glen Grant in 1840; and Glenmorangie in 1842.

The invention of Robert Stein's continuous still in 1828 revolutionized the industry, leading to the mass production of grain whisky and the rise of modern blended Scotch. Rise in levies per proof gallon helped lead to the transcendence of grain whisky. In 1850, malt still ruled, at about 60 percent of the production to grain's 40. Within a decade, those numbers had reversed, and by 1860 most working men drank either grain whisky or a blend.

Drinkers had long noticed that when whisky was allowed to age in cask, it became mellower and smoother in flavor. Merchants began to experiment with aging whiskies in casks, notably old sherry casks, which imparted fruity and nutty flavors to the whisky.

Andrew Usher, in 1853, was the first person known to have blended whiskies to provide a product appealing to a mass audience, smoothing out the rough edges of Highland whiskies with unique, iconoclastic flavors. Strong Highland malts would be mixed with lighter Lowland malts to provide a new product that was rich in character but still mild and smooth.

By the 1880s, the industry was booming, both at home and overseas, helped by a tiny insect that ravaged the French countryside. *Phylloxera vastatrix,* which ate at the roots of grape vines, spread rapidly through France in the 1870s. The bug devastated not only the wine industry but cognac as well. Brandy was up to this point the favored after-dinner drink among the English, but the near ruination of the French brandy industry turned English tastes toward blended Scotch.

Whisky merchants took quickly to London, hoping to capitalize on French misfortune. James Buchanan opened in London in 1879, marketing his Black &

White whisky in the capital. John Walker—or rather his son, Alexander—followed suit the next year. The House of Dewar moved in shortly after, in 1884.

By the end of the century, several blended whiskies were already internationally famous brand names: Buchanan's Black & White, Dewar's, Haig, White Horse, Vat 69, Teacher's, and Johnnie Walker.

But the early 20th century proved hard for the industry. The boom years of the late 19th produced a whisky bubble, with too many brands in the market and too much stock aging in barrels. Prohibition in the United States played a role in shrinking the market for Scotch, as did Temperance movements in England and Scotland. The war years took a toll as well.

However, it was during American Prohibition that Scotch became a prestige drink, the kind you used to impress bosses and friends. Though whisky makers did not even try to penetrate the American market during the Prohibition years, vast quantities entered the United States via Canada, the West Indies, and the Bahamas.

The industry reached a nadir in 1933, when Prohibition and the worldwide depression drove nearly every distillery into mothballs. That year, Glenlivet was one of only 15 in the whole of the country to remain working. The American market, which reopened with Prohibition's end in 1933, again began to provide room for growth.

SCOTCH WHISKY: WHAT IT IS AND HOW TO MAKE IT

The laws regarding Scotch are rather more complex than those regarding Irish whiskey, but it's easy to strip them down into intelligible English. Scotch is made from water and malted barley. If you're making blended Scotch, you can use other cereal grains, such as corn or wheat. If you're making single malt, there's nothing else in there: just malted barley. No barley, no Scotch.

Scotch must be matured in oak casks, in Scotland, for no less than three years. (Note what this *does not say:* It doesn't say used oak bourbon casks or used sherry casks or used port wine casks. Such used casks make the majority of the cooperage that Scotland uses for Scotch production, but they're enshrined only in tradition, not in law.)

Single malt Scotch has a few extra requirements: By definition, it's the product of a single distillery. In other words, you can't mix Scotch from two or more distilleries together and call it "single malt." Single malt is made only from water and barley, with no other grains. Finally, it must be made in pot stills. The grain whiskies in a blended Scotch are made in column stills, but this is not the case with single malts. In other words, if you buy a blended whisky such as Johnnie Walker, the grain whiskies in the blend have been column-distilled, but if you enjoy a single malt such as Glenmorangie, the whisky in the bottle is all pot-distilled.

Makers of single malts will swear to you that pot stills retain more of the character, texture, and flavor of the original mash, whereas column-distilled liquor is closer to pure alcohol, with congeners and other flavor enhancers removed during the distilling process. Most single malts are double distilled in pots, though some get a third distillation pass as well.

Then it's off to the wood. Anything labeled and sold as Scotch whisky needs to be aged in oak casks for at least three years. This is true of every product that carries the "Scotch" name: single malts, single grains, blended malts, blended grains, and blended Scotch. UK law carries no provisions about the source of the casks used to age Scotch. Scotch distillers can use any type of oak cask to age whisky—new or previously used. Distillers can use casks that previously held bourbon, rye, sherry, port, madeira, rum, or brandy, for example. This freedom allows them to manipulate the flavors of Scotch.

Why don't Scotch distillers generally use new barrels? The first reason is economic: Used barrels are cheaper than new ones. Second, new barrels impart stronger woody notes into the flavor and aroma of a whisky. The last reason is innovation: Previously filled casks allow Scotch makers to subtly influence the final character of a whisky. Scotch aged in sherry casks takes on the nutty and floral notes of a great sherry, for example.

SCOTCH REGIONS

Geographically, the world of single malts is divided into five regions, protected by UK law, to ensure that a Scotch labeled with a certain region is actually made in that region. The five regions are Speyside, the Lowlands, the Highlands, Islay, and Campbeltown. Don't invest too much meaning in these regions. Historically, they played a larger role in single malt variations than they do today. When I suggest a certain Scotch for a cocktail recipe, I make the suggestion based not on region but on flavor profile. If you want to know more about the regions, there are many fine books on the topic, including those by Dave Broome and Michael Jackson. (No, not that Michael Jackson.)

HOW TO MIX WITH SCOTCH WHISKY

You're not going to find a lot of cocktail recipes in this book that call for Scotch in any form—not even blended Scotch. It simply doesn't play well with a lot of ingredients. Scotch is a bruiser in a glass, a bully. Vermouth tames it, but generally only sweet red Italian vermouth. A spicy ginger ale—or, even better, a ginger beer—is a good partner. Certain liqueurs work well.

Most of the recipes that do call for Scotch call for blended. Would a single malt work? Some bartenders love using single malts in drinks such as the Rob Roy. I urge you to try it at home. Start with something well-balanced, not too smoky or too light. Glenlivet is good, or Glenfiddich—just to name two possibilities. Also start with something you already know you like. Make a drink and try it.

Scotch isn't the friendliest ingredient in the home bar, but when it works, it really sings. However, if you want something with more versatility, catch a flight to North America. Let's go there now.

RYE WHISKEY

Rye has an interesting story. Although it is the first whiskey made in what became the United States, it nearly fell into complete oblivion, rescued only by the cocktail renaissance of the last 15 years. When I started obsessively studying cocktails and spirits about 12 years ago, rye was conspicuous by its absence. You could hardly find rye anywhere. Today, venerable brands such as Rittenhouse are resurgent, and modern brands are taking shelf space next to the old-timers. Distilleries are ramping up rye production to meet the demand, but they still have some catching up to do.

A SHORT HISTORY OF RYE WHISKEY

The first spirit distilled in the American colonies was almost certainly a fruit brandy, made on stills imported from Scotland and England. It wasn't long, though, before enterprising settlers began building their own stills. The most popular early spirits were peach brandy in the southern colonies, and applejack, or apple brandy, in the north.

By the 1670s, though, the colonies had a new love, and it still wasn't whiskey. It was rum. A thriving trade in molasses from the West Indies began in the mid-1600s, and distillers in New England quickly set up shop to profit from it. Rum's ascendance could only last so long, though. During the revolution, the British blockaded American ports, making it impossible to import molasses for distilling. After the war, Americans distanced themselves from their colonial past, and among other things, this meant avoiding rum. Further, as the new United States expanded westward, people found it too expensive to transport the raw materials for rum making across the mountains and into the new territories.

Some early farmer-distillers tried to grow barley so as to make the Scotches and Irish whiskeys they were familiar with, but they discovered that barley doesn't grow well in North America. They then chose instead to work with local ingredients, especially the grains that grew plentifully around them.

By the 1780s, thousands of farmer-distillers had set up in the woods of Pennsylvania and Maryland. Eventually, various styles of rye whiskey emerged, each pegged to a specific region of the eastern states. Originally, Pennsylvania-style rye, also known as Monongahela rye (named for the Pennsylvania river), was a blast of 100 percent rye. It was a blend of malted and unmalted rye, with no corn or barley. The process of malting rye paralleled the malting process for barley to make Scotch: malting cracks open the grain kernels and starts the process of converting starches to sugars.

By the 20th century, though, Pennsylvania distillers moved from malted rye to malted barley in their mash bills. Anywhere from 80–95 percent was unmalted rye, with malted barley as the remainder. Still no corn. The flavor profile was dry and spicy.

—◦• MGP INGREDIENTS •◦—

Recently, a new style of rye has emerged, almost accidentally, from southeastern Indiana, in a pocket of the state near Ohio and Kentucky. This style emerged from a distillery now owned by MGP Ingredients, a company that makes bulk alcohol. The plant began as a Seagram's distillery making alcohol to blend into its American and Canadian blended whiskeys. Because the alcohol was part of a blend, featuring a mash bill of 95 percent rye and 5 percent malted barley, the output was richly rye-forward. These ryes are rich and spicy and bone dry, not to everyone's taste but certainly to mine.

MGP doesn't bottle any of this rye themselves. Instead, they sell it to other companies, which then age it themselves (in some cases) and bottle it under their own names. Among the ryes from MGP are Templeton, Bulleit, George Dickel, Angel's Envy, and Redemption.

Traditional rye distillers lament the 95-percent recipe, saying it causes people to believe that all rye whiskeys should be 95 percent rye when, in fact, a traditional rye is more like 51 percent.

The other major rye style was Maryland rye. Possessing a softer, fruitier, brighter, and floral style, Maryland rye lives on only in a brand called Pikesville.

This rye used to be hard to find outside Maryland, but in 2015 the brand owner, Heaven Hill, relaunched it nationwide in new packaging.

Most rye distilleries shut down when Prohibition kicked off, never to reopen. Indeed, the Monongahela and Maryland styles are nearly dead, though a few upstart distilleries are monkeying around with reviving those styles. Wish them luck.

A few venerable brands, such as Old Overholt and Rittenhouse, were originally Monongahela ryes. But these were purchased by major distilleries and are now made in Kentucky and feature corn in the mash bill.

RYE WHISKEY: WHAT IT IS AND HOW TO MAKE IT

Rye, like bourbon, must be aged in charred, new oak containers. Why new oak? New oak barrels offer strong flavors and aromas of vanilla, caramel, cocoa, and, well, oakiness. (Scotch producers avoid new barrels because of those very flavors and aromas, which they feel can overpower the subtleties of malt whiskey.)

By law, rye whiskey must contain at least 51 percent rye grain in the mash bill. Some brands go a little higher, into the 60 percent range. Other brands go yet higher (see the sidebar MGP Ingredients). The other grains in the mash are corn and malted barley.

If the rye is labeled as a *straight whiskey,* that means it's at least two years old. If a distiller ages a straight whiskey for less than four years, the distiller is required to list an age statement on the bottle. If you see a straight bourbon or rye without an age statement, it *should* be at least four years old. Unfortunately some distillers play loose with the rules, and the federal government isn't good at policing this. Distillers are allowed to market older spirits with age statements, but generally you don't see this unless the whiskeys are older than about six years.

You don't see many older ryes on the market because the demand for the spirit still outstrips the supply. As a result, most distillers are bottling it after about four years and getting it straight to market.

HOW TO MIX WITH RYE WHISKEY

Aside from perhaps bourbon, rye whiskey is the most mixable spirit in the whiskey world. It goes well with nearly everything. This is one reason for its surge in popularity; bartenders love its versatility.

Try playing with it in mixed drinks. I could have easily filled the book with 75 rye cocktails, but I didn't want rye to hog the show. Check the web if you want to branch out. Sites like Serious Eats, Saveur, Epicurious, and Liquor.com have many rye drink recipes.

GEORGE WASHINGTON

Yes, that *George Washington.*

The first president of the United States was a complicated man—a gentleman farmer, an architect of freedom and a slave owner, a general, a nascent nation's leader and savior, a miller, and a distiller. Washington's Mount Vernon estate comprised more than 5,000 acres at his death in 1799. Washington inherited wealth from his family and managed his finances smartly, making a substantial fortune on his own from growing tobacco.

By the 1760s, however, Washington discerned that tobacco had depleted the soils on his farms, and so he switched to growing grains, notably wheat, corn, and rye. In 1771, he completed work on a gristmill on Dogue Creek, about 5 miles from his mansion, where he produced flour for domestic and overseas markets. Much later in Washington's life, in 1797, his farm manager, a Scotsman named James Anderson, urged him to take his surplus grain, build a distillery, and turn the grain into whiskey. The plan was to sell in Alexandria and Richmond, Virginia. Washington agreed and Anderson immediately constructed the distillery next to the gristmill, making it a simple task to haul newly ground rye, corn, and malted barley to the distillery.

Washington didn't simply distill his own grains, though. He also bought grain from neighboring farmers. The early days of whiskey making—whether in Scotland, Ireland, Virginia, Pennsylvania, or Kentucky—were characterized by farmer-distillers, who made whiskey for their purposes and sold any surplus whiskey they may have had. Washington had a different plan in mind: From the outset, he always meant to sell his whiskey on the open market.

He was smart in another way as well. On the site of the gristmill and distillery, he

also kept pens of hogs. They ate the leftover cooked mash, which helped to fatten them and enrich the flavor of their meat.

Washington's recipe was a lot more rye-forward than most commercial ryes on the market are today. Traditionally, rye mash bills (the recipe of grains in the mix) usually are made of about 51 percent rye, 39 percent corn, and 10 percent barley malt. By contrast, Washington's rye was 60 percent rye, 35 percent corn, and 5 percent barley.

Whiskey was used also as medicine in Washington's time. The swampy Virginia climate bred malaria and other diseases. The water supply was unsafe to drink, and Virginians instead turned to beer, cider, and whiskey to drink.

Archeologists began excavating the original site in the 1990s, and the Mount Vernon Ladies Association (custodians of the Mount Vernon estate) raised the money to rebuild the distillery in 1999, some 200 years after George's death, and opened the new facility in 2007. Today, the distillery makes a small amount of whiskey every year, along with apple and peach brandies, and visitors can see a re-creation of the Washington-Anderson whiskey-making process.

As you approach the distillery, you see wood neatly stacked up in large piles against stone walls of the long, low building. Smoke rises from chimneys in the roof. The distillery smells strongly of pine, oak, and cedar smoke. The distillery uses the wood to fire the stills and boiler. They don't use the smoke to produce malted barley, the way that some barley malt is smoked in Scotland, so the smoke odor doesn't affect the flavor of the whiskey. Nevertheless, when you're in this distillery you're very aware of the smoke.

Steam, too. On one wall of the distillery's interior is a copper boiler, a tub large enough to heat over 200 gallons of water to scalding, stoked by a fire built below. The grains are added to mash tubs, which are large wooden barrels that sit alongside the boiler. Scalding water is carried by bucket to the mash tubs and mixed with the grain to form a kind of porridge. Yeast is added and everything is stirred together to kick-start the fermentation process.

The process is steamy, smoky, and sweaty. Given the high humidity of Virginia, it's easy to recognize just how grueling it is to produce whiskey in this way.

Along the other wall is a row of five copper-pot stills, built on their original foundations, which archaeologists uncovered while digging out the site. The stills are enclosed in brick fire boxes—ovens that trap the heat of the wood fires built beneath each pot.

The pot of each still is topped by a removable bulbous cap, called an "onion" for its shape. When the fermented grainy liquid (almost like a beer) is ready for the still, workers remove the onion, and the "beer" is carried over in buckets. A copper lyne arm descends from the onion, ending in a coil that sits inside a wooden barrel. A

trough of water drawn from Dogue Creek feeds slowly into the barrel, cooling the coil and condensing the hot spirit within. The whiskey runs out the back, where it's collected and filtered before being bottled.

Washington's whiskey was sold "white" or unaged, and in fact this was common practice then. Aging whiskey in oak barrels wasn't a common practice in any form of whiskey (Scotch, bourbon, rye, Irish) until the 19th century. (See the Bourbon Whiskey section on pages 56–64 for details.) This gave Washington an immediate return on his money and made him even wealthier.

Washington died in 1799, just two years after opening his distillery. Anderson, the farm manager, kept it going for another few years, retiring after Martha Washington's death in 1802. George's heir to Mount Vernon failed to manage his properties well, and they fell into disrepair.

At its peak, this was the largest distillery in the United States, producing 11,000 gallons of whiskey and making Washington a profit of $7,500 in 1799 alone (that's about a hundred grand in today's money). The distillery building burned in 1814, but George's writings and other papers preserved knowledge of its operations and a general floor plan for the distillery, which helped archaeologists re-create the distillery in the 21st century.

BOURBON WHISKEY

Today we think of bourbon mainly as the native spirit of the Commonwealth of Kentucky. But the truth about bourbon is that anyone in the United States, from Alaska to Florida, can make it. That's as it should be, because if any spirit is as star-spangled as Captain America, it's bourbon.

A (NOT SO) SHORT HISTORY OF BOURBON WHISKEY

The origins of whiskey distilling in Kentucky are murky and lost to time, mainly because very few historic records of distilling in Kentucky prior to 1800 survive. Kentucky's first settlers were largely illiterate and therefore not given to record keeping.

We might not know the first distiller in Kentucky, but we know some early names. If you're expecting to see Evan Williams and Elijah Craig in the list, I'm going to disappoint you. The brothers Joseph and Samuel Davis are probably not household names in your bourbon cabinet, but when they arrived in Kentucky in 1779, they brought 40-gallon copper pot stills. And the brothers weren't alone.

That same year, 1779, a man named Jacob Meyers arrived in Kentucky and set up a distillery in what is now Lincoln County. You might not know his name, but you know at least the surname of his nephew: Jacob Beam. Jacob was the first Beam to become a distiller, helping out his uncle before setting out on his own.

—•◦• THE BEAMS AND NOES •◦•—

Jacob Beam began distilling around 1792. Nearly 225 years later, his descendants are keeping the faith. The Beams have remained a part of Kentucky bourbon for eight generations and running. Beam descendants today are master distillers at Jim Beam (the now-deceased Booker Noe, his son Fred, and Fred's son Freddie) and at Heaven Hill (Earl Beam, his son Parker, and Parker's son Craig). Every generation of Beams has worked in the industry in some capacity. That's one respectable family legacy.

By 1810, Kentucky had some 2,000 distilleries, reported the historian Thomas D. Clark in his 1937 book A *History of Kentucky*. Most of these, of course, would have been small farm distilleries, mainly noncommercial ones making whiskey for home use and for bartering.

One major question remains: The product these early distillers made—would we recognize it as the bourbon we're familiar with? Probably not. In Kentucky, as in Scotland and Ireland and probably everywhere else, the early history of whiskey is a story of an unaged product that was made quickly and bartered to neighbors for goods and services.

It's not that distillers of the era didn't know how to age whiskey. Cooperage is an old craft, practiced since at least 300 C.E. Distillers knew that leaving whiskey in wooden barrels improved the flavor. They also knew about the process of charring barrels, *and* they knew that aging whiskey in charred barrels improved the flavor even more than in uncharred barrels.

No, the reason farmer-distillers didn't age whiskey was that they didn't need to. They generally sold it as fast as they made it. And since they were already so actively busy making and selling whiskey, they had no compelling reason to age it.

What makes bourbon *bourbon* is the aging process. Bourbon is nothing more or less than an oak-aged, corn-based whiskey. As whiskey and wood interact, chemical compounds in the wood enter into the liquor, changing it forever, giving it color, flavor, and a distinct texture that you cannot find in unaged spirit. Bourbon isn't bourbon without wood.

No one knows who first decided to store whiskey in barrels in Kentucky, but it

was probably not one person, but many of them, and all did this at essentially the same time. As the industry grew, and some farmer-distillers ditched the *farmer* to focus on becoming professional distillers, production capacities expanded. Eventually, distillers had more whiskey than they could immediately sell, and so some of them started to age it.

Another factor in aging whiskey was the growth of the market for good whiskey. In 1802, President Jefferson repealed the unpopular whiskey tax that sparked the Whiskey Rebellion of the 1790s. This, along with his purchase of the Louisiana Territory one year later, opened up vast new markets for Kentucky whiskey. The hooch started going back east, to the original states, and also downriver, along the Kentucky, Ohio, and Mississippi Rivers, to the bustling port town of New Orleans.

From this point on, aging whiskey caught on and became standard. Grocers or other whiskey merchants bought new whiskeys from various distillers, blended them together, and aged them in wood for the purpose of improving the flavor. And indeed, after 1803, the process seemed to have rapidly become popular. "Red"—aged—bourbon is first mentioned in 1821. By the 1850s and 1860s, many accounts of bourbon whiskey refer to it as "red" or "amber" or some other color that implies that it's aged.

One of the major markets for Kentucky whiskey in the 19th century was New Orleans, the former French colony seated on the Mississippi River Delta. Kentucky distillers loaded whiskey onto barges in the Kentucky and Ohio Rivers, sending them down-river to the Mississippi and eventually to Louisiana. French influences in New Orleans extended to drinking. Imbibers in the city were accustomed to wines, brandies, and the finest cognacs. When offered a choice between a mellow, smooth, complex French brandy and a harsh, young Kentucky whiskey, there was no contest.

Distillers and merchants quickly realized that if they wanted to make a profit off of Kentucky whiskey, they'd have to take a cue from the French and age their product. Grocers, pharmacists, and merchants in the Kentucky cities of Lexington, Louisville, and Frankfort would buy new spirit and age it in warehouses before shipping it downriver. Louisville's Main Street, just a short horse-cart ride from the Ohio River, was known for years as Whiskey Row because of the aging warehouses and sales offices that lined the street.

Through the course of the 1800s, the bourbon industry grew and grew. At the same time, new markets for Kentucky's corn and other crops began to emerge. The growth of river shipping and, eventually, the railroad meant a growth in national markets for Kentucky's food crops. Some farmer-distillers ended up focusing on farming, abandoning their stills as their farming business grew. Other farmer-distillers became full-time distillers, purchasing grain from neighbors and eventually forming some of the earliest branded bourbons.

—•• WHISKEY ROW ••—

Main Street, Louisville, is again becoming a Whiskey Row as distilleries open tourism centers there. Heaven Hill's Evan Williams Experience opened in November 2013, and Michter's, Jim Beam, and Brown-Forman are also working on Main Street attractions.

Until the very early years of the 20th century, most bourbon was sold in barrels, directly to liquor stores, merchants or grocers, or bars. Bars, of course, sold it by the glass, and both bars and the other establishments would pour it into crocks, bottles, and other reusable containers brought in by the customer. The distillery's name would be branded with hot iron onto the barrelhead (a practice that continues to this day), with the barrelhead displayed publicly in a bar or store so the consumer could choose a brand.

In 1870, one man changed that: George Garvin Brown. Brown was a pharmaceutical sales representative who traveled frequently, selling pharmaceuticals directly to physicians. At the time, bourbon was still frequently prescribed to patients for various ailments. Doctors told Brown that these whiskeys were inconsistent, in that they were watered down or pumped full of adulterants. Brown saw an opportunity and founded a bourbon brand that would be sold *only* in sealed bottles so as to ensure each drop of bourbon was of consistent high quality. The brand was known as Old Forrester, and it's still marketed today by the company Brown went on to found: Brown-Forman (which also owns Jack Daniel's, among many other products). Today, however, the brand has only one *r*, and goes by Old Forester. No one's quite sure why the brand lost an *r*.

Brown was the first to bottle his bourbon, and for a while he was the only one. It's not that bottles were unavailable; they were just too expensive for most distillers to use. It wasn't until the early years of the 20th century that technology improved enough for distillers to economically ship bourbon in bottles.

Bourbon rode high in the late 19th and early 20th centuries, but then the bottom dropped out when the Volstead Act of 1919 regulated the manufacture and sale of beverage alcohol. Most distilleries closed outright and never reopened, not even after the repeal of Prohibition in 1933. A small few used a government loophole to remain open, making whiskey for medicinal purposes. Doctors and pharmacists were legally allowed to prescribe whiskey, and the government granted licenses to a few distilleries to remain open for the purpose of meeting this market. (And a large market it was, as suddenly millions of American developed maladies they'd never had prior to Prohibition.)

With repeal, the need arose for distilleries to reopen. Those that remained open under medicinal license ramped up production, whereas new distilleries also began to crop up. Heaven Hill, which currently produces Evan Williams bourbon and Rittenhouse Rye, formed, for example, in 1935. But the process was slow. Whiskey, of course, is an aged product, which meant that new or newly reopened distilleries couldn't simply make the product and immediately sell it. They had to enter the business slowly and deliberately.

Because of this, American whiskey was just starting to get its legs back when something happened to knock those legs out from under it again: World War II. The war effort required copious amounts of industrial alcohol for use in making antifreeze, plastics, synthetic rubber, and ammunition. It wasn't until after the war ended that the bourbon industry began to recover. The post-war economic boom breathed new life into the industry. Service members who remained in the Armed Forces in post-war assignments in Western Europe and Japan spread the word about American whiskey. The global ascendance of such brands as Jack Daniel's and Jim Beam began this way, as American servicemen drank them while off duty.

The late 1940s and the 1950s were great years for American whiskey, but another hazard loomed on the horizon.

NOT YOUR FATHER'S INTOXICANTS

American whiskey's lot began to fall in the 1960s and 1970s, as Baby Boomers started coming of age and rebelling against the intoxicants of their parents. Whiskey—all whiskey, not just American—was seen as an old fogey's drink. It was not something hip and young and trendy. And recall that the 1960s also brought with them a rise in the use of other mind-altering substances. The young people of the '60s and '70s chose to turn on, tune in, and drop out, and did so without a drop of bourbon or Scotch.

Not to say that the only mind-altering substances of this era were illegal drugs. There also occurred a dramatic rise in vodka consumption. Much of vodka's appeal stemmed from its association with the Soviet Union, and therefore vodka held a countercultural appeal during the height of the Cold War. Bourbon and rye, being such iconic American tipples, were the drink of The Man, and therefore were to be shunned.

Bourbon responded by slimming down. At the beginning of the '70s, many bourbon and rye brands were bottled at 100 proof. To reach consumers who preferred lighter flavors, whiskey makers dropped the proof on nearly all major brands from 100 to 90, from 90 to 86, and eventually from 86 to 80, the legal minimum. Plants closed, brands left the market (perhaps forever), and people lost jobs they thought they'd hold until retirement. A dim era for American whiskey.

One light that still shone brightly for the industry in this period was the export market. Bourbon was still flying off the shelves in Japan and parts of Europe. In America, Maker's Mark, after it was profiled on the front page of the *Wall Street Journal*, finally started to find an audience again, after decades of slow growth.

What most ignited American whiskey, though, was the single malt Scotch craze of the 1980s. For all of Scotch's history, blended Scotch had outsold single malts by vast amounts. But in the '80s, Americans began to see single malts as a symbol of upward mobility—something to drink after you've "made it" in business.

Booker Noe, at Jim Beam, saw this and decided to cut in on Scotch, creating the Small Batch Bourbon Collection. Booker's bourbon was its first release, in 1987, blasting opening a new market for super-premium bourbons.

BOURBON WHISKEY: WHAT IT IS AND HOW TO MAKE IT

If you want to make bourbon, you need to follow a few rules that have been set out by the United States government and enshrined into law. In all likelihood, you already know that bourbon is made mainly of corn. In fact, by law the blend of grains used in bourbon must contain at least 51 percent corn. The remaining 49 percent of the blend is up to the maker, though it is usually some mix of wheat, rye, malted rye, and malted barley. The exact recipe depends on the flavor profile the distiller is looking for.

WHY BOURBON?

I mentioned earlier that bourbon is nothing more or less than an oak-aged, corn-based whiskey. Once it acquired the wood, how did it get the name? No one knows.

Sure, sure. You'll hear a guy some night at your local bar telling everyone in earshot that bourbon is called bourbon because it's made in Bourbon County, Kentucky. Maybe you've even been that guy. I wish it were that simple because then we could move on and forget about it. Alas, it's not. Once upon a time, Bourbon County housed distilleries, sure, and maybe the name arises from that fact. But today, not a single whiskey distillery exists in the modern borders of Bourbon County. So Bar Guy needs a new tall tale to tell.

I've seen a lot of claims and possible explanations about the origins of the name. Bourbon historian Michael Veach posits that it was called *bourbon* to make it more marketable in French-influenced New Orleans. After all, the House of Bourbon was a lineage of famous French kings, and a product that sounds like it may have been named for them should sell well to people who still identify with their French homeland, right?

Another whiskey historian, Henry Crowgey, puts up a slightly different story. What is now Bourbon County is merely a tiny fraction of the original Bourbon County. Back in its earliest days, Kentucky wasn't a separate state, but a district of Virginia. As a way to thank the French government for supplying the American Revolution with arms, money, and soldiers, the Virginia legislature named several counties in the new Kentucky district after French families. Bourbon County, Virginia, was established in 1785 as a vast region, encompassing dozens of today's counties. In that region was a small port town, Maysville, located in the northern part of Kentucky, on the Ohio River.

For decades after Bourbon County was partitioned into smaller and smaller counties, the entire region continued to be known as Old Bourbon. Whiskey from throughout the region would travel via horse to Maysville, where the barrels would be stenciled with the words "Old Bourbon Whiskey" to indicate its region of origin—that is, whiskey from Old Bourbon. Over time, as people stopped referring to the region as Old Bourbon, the younger generations naturally but incorrectly assumed that the Old referred to bourbon whiskey that had aged for a long time.

Confused? That's okay, so are all of us who write about whiskey professionally. At this point, there's just no way to prove any of the stories about how bourbon came to be called *bourbon*.

Bourbon must, by law, be aged in charred, new-oak containers. Note that word, *containers.* In practice, nearly all bourbon is aged in barrels made from charred, new American white oak (*Quercus alba*, if you're interested), from the eastern United States. Whiskey makers have used white oak for as long as they've been aging bourbon because of the smells and flavors this wood imparts into the bourbon. Consumers expect those qualities, and so I don't expect bourbon makers to change this practice.

—•• SOUR MASH ••—

Today, when you look at a bottle of bourbon, you'll often see the words "Sour Mash" on the label. This refers to a process by which yeast is added to the fermentation tank. In this regard, distillers have two options: sweet mash and sour mash.

Sweet mash involves cooking grain and adding yeast to the mash in the fermentation tank, which is essentially the process behind making Irish whiskey and Scotch. Sour mash uses liquid from a previous distillation in the new mash. This provides consistency from batch to batch and makes the mash more acidic, which in turn prevents bacteria from spoiling the mash.

It's that acidity in the mash that inspired the name *sour mash*—it's sour in the same way that lactic acid makes fermented food, such as sauerkraut, taste sour.

WHEAT WHISKEY

Wheat whiskey is just like bourbon or rye, except that instead of requiring 51 percent corn or rye, it requires 51 percent wheat, by law. The only major-label brand on the market is Heaven Hill Bernheim. Don't confuse wheat whiskey with a so-called wheated bourbon. A wheated bourbon is still at least 51 percent corn, but instead of having rye as the secondary flavor grain, a wheated bourbon uses wheat. Maker's Mark is the best known wheated bourbon on the market.

HOW TO MIX WITH BOURBON WHISKEY

Bourbon is a remarkably versatile spirit for cocktails. It pairs well not just with liqueurs, juices, bitters, and sugar, but also with other brown spirits, such as rum and brandy.

One thing to note, though: Many of the bourbon recipes in this book were devised at a time when most bourbons on the market were bottled at 100 proof.

Today, most bourbon is bottled at 80 proof. You can still get higher-proof bourbons, and I recommend them for mixing. Wild Turkey 101 is a great mixing bourbon. Jim Beam recently released a 100-proof version of its flagship Beam brand, specifically because bartenders requested it.

Look for anything "bottled in bond," which has specific legal requirements that set it apart from traditional bourbon. The only thing you really need to know about so-called bonded bourbons is that they are always bottled at 100 proof.

Barring that, look for bourbons at 90 proof and 86 proof, which are also good for mixing.

TENNESSEE WHISKEY

Tennessee whiskey is a bit of an odd category. In fact, I might argue it's not even a separate category at all. Tennessee whiskey, you see, is straight bourbon that is produced with an extra step: charcoal filtering. And until recently, only two distilleries in the state even produced Tennessee whiskey at all: Jack Daniel's and George Dickel.

A SHORT HISTORY OF TENNESSEE WHISKEY

Tennessee's distillation history is perhaps unsurprisingly similar to Kentucky's, considering that they're neighboring states. As was true with its northern cousin, settlers to Tennessee began distilling almost as soon as they put down roots in their new home. The first distillery on record opened in 1771, and by the 1790s, distillation had spread throughout Tennessee.

Not long after, the temperance movement began in the state, with the first formal temperance society starting in 1829. The movement continued to grow through the 19th century. The country's first prohibition law, in fact, was enacted in Tennessee in 1838, banning the sale of alcohol in taverns and stores. The crime was merely a misdemeanor, punishable by fine, and the law was overturned in 1846.

The Civil War put a brief halt to the industry. Occupying Union forces shut down the stills to divert grain to feed people and livestock. As soon as the Union forces left, however, the distilleries started working again. The industry grew in the remaining years of the 18th century, with the temperance movement growing right alongside it. By the 1880s, beverage alcohol was the largest industry in the state, but at the same time, legislation was passed that essentially banned liquor outside of the largest cities in the state.

In 1909, the hammer dropped: The legislature passed a law banning all production of alcoholic beverages in the state. Every distillery immediately shut down, some 11 years before national Prohibition went into effect. By 1917, it was illegal to even possess liquor or transport it into or out of the state.

Though Prohibition was repealed in 1933, Tennessee passed a law six years later that allowed local communities to control the sale and consumption of alcohol in their boundaries, a law that holds to this day. As a result, about a third of the state is completely dry.

The Cascade distillery (now George Dickel) and Jack Daniel's were the only pre-Prohibition distilleries to reopen after repeal. Until Pritchard's Distillery opened in 1997, they were the only two in the state. Lately, a few smaller distilleries have started up, offering their own take on Tennessee whiskey.

TENNESSEE WHISKEY: WHAT IT IS AND HOW TO MAKE IT

What distinguishes Tennessee whiskey from bourbon? Not much, actually. Jack Daniel's and George Dickel are each a sour mash product, made mostly from corn, with a mix of grains that includes wheat, rye, and malted barley. The grains are ground, mixed with water, and fermented in a method similar to that of bourbon. The fermented liquid is distilled in a column still before being aged in new, charred-oak barrels.

The only difference is something called the *Lincoln County Process*, in which new-make (or white dog) whiskey is filtered through a tall column of sugar maple charcoal chips prior to aging. The whiskey filters through this vat from top to bottom before it's aged. The charcoal is said to mellow out the flavor of the whiskey, smoothing its rough edges, and producing a softer, drier liquor. In a way, this process kickstarts the aging process.

HOW TO MIX WITH TENNESSEE WHISKEY

Like bourbon, Tennessee whiskey is versatile for bartenders and easy to mix with, though the lack of a higher-proof Tennessee presents something of a challenge. As with bourbon, an 80-proof Tennessee can get lost in certain cocktails. Dickel offers a 90-proof release; use that if you can find it.

AMERICAN CRAFT WHISKEYS

One thing I need to immediately get out of the way when discussing craft whiskey is that there's no such thing as craft whiskey—or, more accurately, there's no legal definition of the term. "Craft" means whatever a whiskey maker wants it to mean. Diageo, the world's biggest producer of alcoholic beverages, recently signaled itself as a "craft" distiller.

The only answer here is: do your homework. Say you see a cool-looking whiskey bottle in your local spirits boutique. Maybe the boozemongers know something about the bottle, and maybe they don't. Doesn't hurt to ask. Bring it home, taste it, decide whether you like it. If you like it, the biggest part of your homework assignment is finished.

Want extra credit? Google the brand and find its website. Chances are strong that if the brand owners work on-site making the product—or ever have at some point in the past—the website will have photos of their stills, their barrels, and maybe their bottling line. The "About" page might have charming stories of how the owners gave up careers in finance or publishing or real estate or medicine or landscape gardening or whatever to open the distillery of their dreams. Do they give tours? If they actually let you see the stills, they probably don't have much to hide.

If they're super-transparent, they'll even have a mission statement or some sort of idea of their future business plan. You see, making whiskey is a costly process, especially if you're an honest person planning to make straight whiskey. Remember, straight whiskey is at least two years old, and that means opening a distillery, making whiskey, barreling it, and *making no money whatsoever for two long years*.

Many independent whiskey producers start with gin, vodka, liqueurs, or "white whiskey" or "moonshine"—that is, their whiskey distillate sold without any age on it. They sell that to get some cash flow while waiting for the whiskey to age. With these producers, it's easy to tell what their plan is, and most of them will talk enthusiastically about their current products and with great zeal about what's in the pipeline.

Other producers buy whiskey to sell under their own name while waiting for their own product to age. Some of these producers, like Utah's High West or West Virginia's Smooth Ambler, are perfectly up front about it. If you encounter their brands, you're lucky. The stuff they're buying to resell is all very good, and the stuff they're making themselves is also quite good.

Other such producers are really secretive. The whiskey they sell might be delicious and therefore still worth buying, but they gussy it up in stories about how it was Al Capone's favorite recipe, when that's not possible considering the actual recipe was invented in Southern Indiana in the 1980s.

So the point is, do your homework and see how open the makers are about what they're doing. And if you like the brand, you can decide for yourself whether it's "craft."

The true craft distillers, though, are where much of the innovation in whiskey is happening today. They're the ones making spirit from spelt, quinoa, triticale. They're the ones using blue corn for bourbon or aging whiskey in French-oak casks. They're smoking their barley with peat from Louisiana marshes to make an American spin on single malt barley whiskey.

If you like these whiskeys and you want to mix with them, then do so. You might find however that their peculiarities are hard to work with in traditional cocktails. No matter; these distillers will have recipes on their websites or in their promotional materials, and chances are good they found a talented bartender to devise cocktails that befit the whiskey's flavor profile. Don't be afraid to have some fun with these.

CANADIAN WHISKY

Whiskey, whisky. Call it whatever you want, just remember to send me a bottle. Canada takes more than just its spelling from Scotland; it also takes much of its philosophy. Most Canadian whisky is blended, a mix of grain whisky and flavoring whiskies. Canadian whisky has an unfortunate reputation for being "brown vodka." Though this might accurately describe *some* of the Great White North's output, it is nevertheless an unfair description for most of the fine bottlings Canadian distilleries are producing today. In fact, Canadian whisky has a smooth, mild profile that allows it to mix well in cocktails, especially if you tailor the cocktail to suit the spirit.

A SHORT HISTORY OF CANADIAN WHISKY

Early distillation in Canada followed some of the same patterns of its southern neighbor: Early settlers to the land brought stills with them from Scotland and Ireland. What's surprising, though, is that those settlers weren't making whisky. They were making rum. As settlers moved west across the continent, however, it became harder and harder to get access to Caribbean molasses, and so they switched to distilling grain-based products.

The original Canadian style was a wheat-based style, since wheat grows so plentifully on the Canadian plains. German and Dutch immigrants, however, liked a spicier style, and they began incorporating rye grain into the whisky. To differentiate this from the common, wheaty style, they referred to the whisky as "rye," though this does not mean now, and did not mean then, that rye is the dominant grain. Nevertheless, when Canadian whisky makers started using rye as a flavoring grain, Canadian whisky picked up the nickname *rye whisky*.

CANADIAN WHISKY: WHAT IT IS AND HOW TO MAKE IT

The base of most Canadian whisky is a high-proof grain spirit, mostly neutral in flavor and essentially identical to the grain whiskies that Scotch blenders use. It provides the bulk of the volume of the finished whisky. The flavoring whisky is distilled out to a much lower proof and it's much richer in flavor.

Canadian whisky makers don't use mash bills, per se—unlike their American and Scottish counterparts, who do use them. In American bourbon production, for example, distillers make a "mash" of grains—usually corn, wheat, and rye—and ferment and distill the grains together. By contrast, Canadian distillers keep every grain separate throughout the production process—mashing, fermenting, distilling, and aging—and only mix the liquids together just before bottling. (There are exceptions, but even these makers keep everything separate up until the aging process, where they blend the distillates together before aging.)

This is not to say that blends are all that Canada produces. On the contrary, distilleries up North also make the Canadian equivalent of straight whisky, with no grain alcohol at all. These tend to be rich, flavorful whiskies, great in drinks such as the Old Fashioned (pages 123–125) or the Whiskey Sour (page 109).

Canadian whisky needs to be aged for at least three years, though the law doesn't make any requirements as to whether the barrels need to be used or new. In practice, most distillers use former bourbon barrels, though in his book *Tasting Whiskey*, Lew Bryson reports that some distillers are experimenting with new barrels and other woods, such as red oak, to see how they affect flavor.

HOW TO MIX WITH CANADIAN WHISKY

Canadian whisky is like Scotch in that you have to find a robust-tasting blend. Entry-level blends are generally too light to mix well with other ingredients. A relatively recent import to the United States is the Dark Batch release from Alberta Distillers. It's rich and tasty, with good rye notes and a robust complexity. It mixes very well in cocktails. Canadian Club has a 100-percent rye on the market. Crown Royal has a rye-heavy release, as does J. P. Wiser's.

JAPANESE WHISKY

The Japanese broadcaster NHK offers a morning drama, known in Japan as *asadora*. Aimed at housewives, the *asadora* airs for 15 minutes, six mornings a week at eight o'clock. The stories always revolve around a woman and the challenges she faces raising a family or establishing a career. Unlike American soap operas, the stories have a beginning and an ending. Each *asadora* airs for just a few months before another, with a new cast and storyline, takes its place. The stories are often historical fiction, set, for example, in postwar Japan or in the 19th century. Often, they're based on real-life figures, but with a fictionalized veneer.

In late 2014, NHK made history by casting the first non-Japanese woman to play an *asadora* lead, in a story called *Massan*. American actress Charlotte Kate Fox played Ellie Kameyama, the Scottish wife of Masaharu Kameyama (whom Ellie nicknames Massan). In the drama, Ellie and Masaharu meet in Scotland in the early 1900s while Masaharu attends graduate school there, studying chemistry. Masaharu develops an interest in Scotch whisky during his studies. (He's hardly the first or last to develop an interest in booze during grad school.) The *asadora* follows the couple as they return to Japan where Massan establishes a career in developing and refining the Japanese whisky industry, and Ellie adapts to life in a new country.

A BRIEF HISTORY OF JAPANESE WHISKY

The Kameyamas are based on a real couple, Masataka Taketsuru and his Scottish wife, Rita Cowan Taketsuru. The bones of the story told in *Massan* are accurate. Masataka Taketsuru grew up in a sake-making family, where he learned that sake production is both art and science. To hone his understanding of the science, he became a chemist. After discovering Scotch whisky, however, he found a new vocation. And so he traveled to Scotland in 1918 to study organic chemistry at the University of Glasgow. He met Rita while taking up lodging in her family's home. He also apprenticed for the Longmorn and Hazelburn distilleries, where he learned how to blend whiskies to make superb Scotches.

In 1920, Taketsuru married Rita. They moved to Japan, where he went to work for Kotobukiya, later known as Suntory, to build Japan's first whisky distillery at Yamazaki. He later opened his own distillery, Nikka, at Yoichi. Suntory and Nikka today are Japan's two top whisky companies.

The Suntory story starts in 1899, when Shinjiro Torii set out to introduce Western-style spirits and wines to the Japanese market. Rather than importing them, as Japan had done for ages, Torii decided to make them himself in Japan. He worked on wines first, and then in 1921, with Taketsuru's help, opened Yamazaki.

Whisky has long played a role in Japanese culture, and not just releases from Scotland and Japan. Bourbon brands are popular there as well, and Japanese firms currently own two American whiskey companies. For many years, the best-selling American whiskey in Asia was Four Roses, marketed there as a straight bourbon. This same whiskey was marketed in the United States as a bottom-shelf, rotgut blended whiskey. In 2001, the Kirin Brewing Company (a member of the Mitsubishi group of companies) purchased Four Roses from Seagram's, and gradually reintroduced this straight bourbon in the American market.

Suntory purchased Beam Inc. for $16 billion in 2014, acquiring at the time not just the entire Jim Beam family of whiskeys but also Maker's Mark bourbon. The new firm, Beam Suntory, now has an international portfolio of whiskeys, including Beam's bourbons and ryes, Maker's Mark, Canadian Club, several Irish whiskeys, and three single malt Scotches: Ardmore, Bowmore, and Laphroiag. Shinjiro Torii's company has gone international.

In July 2015, I was invited to taste a new whisky release from Suntory's Hibiki line. In addition to tasting the final product, the journalists in attendance also got to taste five of the component whiskies. Those five whiskies were quite different from one another.

First up was a grain whisky from Suntory's Chita distillery. This was delicate and flowery, with very subtle flavors of caramel, oak, and vanilla. Next was a whisky aged in used American white oak barrels, previously used for bourbon. Not surprisingly, this whisky reminded me somewhat of bourbon: chocolate on the nose with dried fruit and, well, bourbon flavors on the palate. A sherry-casked aged whisky tasted like raisins, while a whisky aged in Japanese mizunara-wood casks reminded me of sandalwood and musk. Rounding out the five was a smoky malt reminiscent of Scotland's Ardbeg. The finished product blended these five whiskies with other, undisclosed whiskies to produce a light, easily drinkable blend with hints of the individual whiskies in the mix.

JAPANESE WHISKY: WHAT IT IS AND HOW TO MAKE IT

Generally speaking, Japanese whisky is made in a Scotch style, but with Japanese touches. One thing that sets Japanese whisky apart from bourbon or Scotch, however, is that Japanese distilleries generally make several different kinds of whisky. These then get blended together in various ways to make the final product.

Contrast this approach with bourbon: Bourbon makers make bourbon and nothing else. When, say, Wild Turkey fires up its fermentation tanks and stills, it's making one recipe of bourbon, in the same way, each and every time, from the same mix of grains and the same yeast strain. Everything goes into new American white oak barrels—just one type of barrel from one type of wood. When it's time to bottle up the Kickin' Chicken, the blenders at Wild Turkey take samples from barrels stored around the various warehouses to batch them together to make a product that tastes like Wild Turkey's traditional style.

Scotch takes a different approach. Blended Scotches are made by taking single malts from a variety of distilleries and mixing them together to make a Scotch that tastes like, say, the famous Johnnie Walker flavor profile.

Japan whisky making doesn't work this way. What Japanese manufacturers have chosen to do is to make a variety of whisky styles in-house and then blend them together in just the right proportion to produce a whisky that matches the house style.

Yamazaki, for example, uses different types of yeast, different types of fermentation tanks, different shapes of pot still, a variety of grains, and different types of barrels to create and age its whiskies. Each whisky has a unique profile, and these are batched together to create the blends that Yamazaki sends to market.

Japanese producers have to do it this way because they can't swap barrels with each other the way that Scotch producers can.

HOW TO MIX WITH JAPANESE WHISKY

Finding a mixable Japanese whisky is a little tough right now. Japanese producers were as caught off guard by the whiskey boom as were distillers everywhere. So a decade ago, when, say, Yamazaki was laying down supplies of whisky for its 12-year-old release, they couldn't have guessed that sales of Japanese whisky were about to skyrocket.

The demand for Japanese whisky outstrips the supply at present, and that's driving prices up to the point where it's hard to find a bottling that's affordable enough for mixed drinks. Five years ago, you could find an ample supply of bottles under $40, but doing so today is much harder. Suntory and Nikka are working on getting lower-priced products into the American market, so I hope they are able to do so.

This price pressure, though, has made it hard to find more than just a couple of Japanese-whisky cocktails for this book.

WORLD WHISKIES

The world of whisky largely centers on Scotland, Ireland, the United States, Canada, and Japan. But these are hardly the only whisky-making nations in the world. (Every distillery mentioned in this section is inspired by the Scotch-whisky style, so I've chosen to call them all by the name *whisky*, without the *e*.)

Staying in the British Isles, you can find Penderyn single malt Welsh whisky; the English whisky companies St. George's Distillery, in Norfolk; the Lakes Distillery, in Cumbria; and finally the London Distillery Company.

Ride the train through the Channel Tunnel into France, and you'll find Allison Patel's Brenne whisky, a single malt aged first in new French Limousin oak barrels and then finished in used cognac barrels. Bastille 1789 takes its name from the history books; it's a wheat and barley whisky that is aged in French Limousin barrels and other casks. France produces a number of other whiskies as well, but they're mainly available only in Europe.

Elsewhere in Europe, the countries of Germany, Finland, the Netherlands, Spain, and Sweden also offer whiskies. From there, let's move east into Asia. You'll find Amrut in India, making Scotch-inspired Indian single malts for the vast and quickly growing Indian market. Though China is also a quickly growing market for whisky, no major brands are currently produced there. Taiwan, however, offers Kavalan, an excellent whisky producer. Head south of the equator, and you'll find whiskies from New Zealand, Australia, and South Africa.

Many of these distilleries are relatively new, founded within the last 10 years, since the whisky boom started in earnest. Supplies of imported whisky in some countries are so tight right now that it just makes sense for entrepreneurs in those nations to make the stuff right at home and avoid the scramble to bring it in from abroad.

Chapter 3

HOW TO MAKE A COCKTAIL

This chapter will discuss the techniques and equipment you'll need to mix a good cocktail. I'll describe the glassware, mixing tools, ingredients, and other stuff you'll need to whip up drinks at home.

EQUIPMENT

Before you go buying whiskey, equip yourself with a few basic tools.

SHAKERS AND MIXING GLASSES

The first things you'll need to buy are mixing vessels: an easy-to-use cocktail shaker and a mixing glass. Shakers are available in two types—the cobbler shaker and the Boston shaker.

- **Cobbler shaker:** You can find this kind of cocktail shaker in nearly any housewares store; it's the three-piece "classic" style that you've probably seen before: all-metal with a body, perforated top, and little cap that fits over the perforated area. I hate these things. Thanks to the all-metal construction, the pieces seize up when they're cold, making it hard to open for cleaning or reuse.

- **Boston shaker:** A Boston shaker consists of a shaking tin and a mixing glass. They're relatively inexpensive, and lately they're getting a lot easier to find. By building your cocktail in the mixing glass you can watch what you're doing as you add ingredients. As a result, you'll be less likely to mismeasure or forget an ingredient. A Boston shaker does require a separate strainer, but that means you can choose the proper strainer for the given task.

- **Mixing glass:** I usually just use the glass that comes with the Boston shaker set I'm using, though you can buy the glasses stand-alone, too. Professional bartenders like tempered glass, because they can take a just-used glass, still cold from the ice, and drop it into a hot, soapy sink, without worrying about it breaking. You can look for that if you want, but I doubt most home bartenders need tempered glass.

When do you use the shaker, and when do you use the mixing glass? Check in at "When Should I Stir and When Should I Shake?" on pages 81–82.

JIGGERS AND MEASURING CUPS

Measuring tools are important in drink making for the same reason they are important in cooking and baking. You want to be sure you have the right amount of ingredients in your drinks in order to produce a consistent result every time. Do you want your next Blood and Sand (page 155) to taste as delicious as the previous one? Then measure. Unless you're very skilled at free-pouring—and very few beginners are—there's no way you'll pour the correct amount of Scotch, cherry brandy, vermouth, and orange juice each and every time without measuring. To measure, you can use either jiggers or small measuring cups:

- Jiggers are the basic hourglass-shaped stainless-steel measuring devices you've seen in many a bar. These are cheap and easy to find, but I must be honest: I never use a jigger at home. First of all, not all jiggers are equal. Some that might appear to measure a true jigger actually measure 1¼ ounces instead of 1½. If I want accuracy in my measuring (and I do), I don't want to have to second-guess the capacity of my tools.

- My measurer of choice is the Oxo mini angled measuring cup. I love this darned thing, and I use it daily. I only have one problem with it: there's no mark for ¾ of an ounce. I usually eyeball it, or if I need more precision, I measure ½ and then a ¼ ounce.

I should point out, too, that I use ounces for the measures in my recipes in this book. By contrast, some publications provide measurements in cup increments. The recipes in this book say, for example, "2 ounces rye whiskey," whereas other publications would say "¼-cup rye whiskey." These are equivalent measures, and I am aware that most people are more likely to have a ¼-cup measurer around than they are to have one delineated in ounces. But we're making drinks here, so we're going with ounces.

I always recommend that you measure and pour your ingredients into the shaker or mixing glass without ice. This allows you to watch what you're doing so that you can keep track of your ingredients and avoid over- or under-pouring. There's another advantage: if you build the drink without ice, you can step away, if necessary, and not have the ice melt into the cocktail while it awaits your return to stir or shake.

STRAINERS

When shopping for strainers, you need a tool that will let you get the drink out of the shaker and into your glass—preferably without bits of herb and chips of ice. There are a couple of common types:

- A julep strainer has a perforated bowl-shaped cup and an attached handle. It fits well into a mixing glass, and it's useful for straining stirred drinks such as Manhattans (pages 120–122) and Sazeracs (pages 136–137).

- A Hawthorne strainer consists of a flat disk with a coiled spring attached to it. The spring traps ice chips and other solid ingredients, such as muddled fruit or mint leaves. Hawthornes are typically used when straining shaken cocktails from mixing tins, and the spring allows you to control the flow of liquid from the shaker.

If you can only buy one, buy the Hawthorne: The control of the spring makes it the more versatile of the two types. Oh, and why's the other called a "julep strainer," you ask? Originally, a smaller version of today's strainer was used to serve juleps, prior to the widespread introduction of the drinking straw. The julep strainer held the ice and mint back in the glass while the drinker sipped the cocktail.

BAR SPOON

A bar spoon has an obvious purpose: stirring. But why do you need a special tool for that? A bar spoon is specially designed for stirring cocktails. Its long neck reaches the bottom of even the largest mixing glass, and its shape allows the spoon to spin freely in your stirring hand while it moves around the glass. Not all bar spoons, though, are worth buying. Avoid getting the cheap kind with the red plastic cap on the end. The caps invariably fall off, leaving a poky end that can injure your hand.

You can find spoons with twisted shafts or straight ones. Just look for a spoon with a good balance, a decent heft, and a comfortable fit in your hand.

PARING KNIFE

A well-equipped home bar needs just two knives: a paring knife and a chef's knife. A great paring knife is a home bartender's best friend. In the kitchen, a paring knife may be second in command behind a chef's knife, but the opposite is true come cocktail hour.

I use my paring knife for a variety of home bar tasks: cutting swaths of zest for twisting over cocktails; cutting lime wheels and citrus wedges; prepping slices of apple or pear to perch on the rim of a glass; trimming leaves off berries for use in syrups and homemade cordials; and trimming herbs or other savory garnishes.

CHEF'S KNIFE

A well-made chef's knife is crucial for working with large fruit like pineapples, and for cutting citrus in half prior to juicing. If you can afford to do so, I suggest buying a separate knife just for your bar so that it doesn't pick up food odors and stays sharp longer.

CHANNEL KNIFE

I said that only two knives are essential for cocktail work, and that's true. But a channel knife makes a nice add-on, and it's not usually too expensive. If I want a long, thin, curly twist of citrus zest, I'll use a channel knife. If you want the freedom to be creative with your garnishes, a channel knife is handy.

CITRUS JUICERS

Stores are full of gadgets that will help you juice citrus. But for my needs, a simple hand squeezer is good enough. I'm currently using a squeezer made by a company called Chef'n. The geared hinge provides a little more force than many other hand squeezers offer, and the handle is quite comfortable in the hand. It accommodates both lemons and limes, and it can take a small orange or tangerine, too.

GLASSWARE

Though your local housewares store probably carries enough types of glassware to make your eyes glaze over, you really only need four different types of glasses. They will contain nearly any cocktail you might want to make:

- Stemmed, or up, glasses
- Old-fashioned, or rocks, glasses
- Chimney-style glasses (that is, highball or collins glasses)
- Champagne flutes

You might also want to get these:

- Mint julep cup
- Irish coffee mug
- Regular coffee mug

How do you know which glass to use with which drink? Use a stemmed glass whenever you're serving a prechilled drink without any ice in the glass. Instead of holding the glass by its bowl, which would warm the drink, you hold it by the stem and raise it to your waiting lips. Use an old-fashioned glass for drinks that are built in the glass (meaning you're not using a cocktail shaker or mixing glass—you're mixing the drink, usually with ice, in the serving glass). Use a highball glass when you're sipping something cold and refreshing that's served over lots of ice, sometimes with a straw.

There is one exception to these rules: the Sazerac (pages 136–137). This drink is served prechilled, in a rocks glass, without ice. This is simply the tradition in New Orleans: The drink is served as a 2-ounce pour that most drinkers finish before it warms up too much. If you're concerned, you can chill the glass in the freezer before you drink.

You've probably seen a few different types of stemmed glasses. Most common is the iconic V-shaped glass (sometimes called a martini glass). It has a drawback, though, as you probably know if you've had a little too much to drink: It's easy to tip over. Its lesser-known cousin—the coupe glass—doesn't have that problem. The coupe started life as a champagne glass, but drinkers soon found the coupe is not all that well suited to champagne. Its shape causes the bubbles to evaporate before the wine reaches the mouth. But the coupe is very well adapted for cocktails! I like having both types of stemware on hand. I reserve the V-shaped cocktail glass for a classic martini. Everything else suited for stemware goes into a coupe: Manhattans, Brooklyns, Rob Roys, you name it.

Making tall, cool drinks served over ice? The chimney-style glass that you need goes by a few different names: the delmonico, the collins, and the highball. The delmonico is the smallest of the chimney styles at 5 to 8 ounces; the highball rings in at about 8 to 12 ounces; and the collins comes in at 12 to 16 ounces. Historically, they were each used for a different type of cocktail. You'll still find bartenders who insist on serving a Tom Collins in a collins glass, but a gin fizz in a highball. For home use, I think these distinctions are unnecessary. If I had to choose only one, I'd take the middle ground and go with the 10-ounce highball glass.

SMALLER IS BETTER (THOUGH HARDER TO FIND)

One thing I hate about shopping for cocktail glasses: they're all so damn big. Chain stores mainly stock stemmed glasses in the 10 to 15 ounce range; double old-fashioned glasses reach 14 ounces; and highballs go up to 20 ounces. These aren't cocktail glasses; they're swimming pools. (Ahhhh, to swim in bourbon . . .)

Nearly all the recipes in this book call for 3 or so ounces of liquid, unless they're highballs. To make the recipes here, then, I generally recommend seeking out the following size glasses:

- Stemmed (V or coupe): 5 to 7 ounces
- Old-fashioned or rocks: 6 to 8 ounces; double: 12 to 14 ounces
- Chimney-style: 10 to 16 ounces

TECHNIQUE

When you mix a cocktail, you have three main goals:

- Blending the ingredients
- Diluting the drink to the ideal level of dilution
- Chilling the drink to its ideal temperature

I'll look at each of these techniques in turn. Now, it's pretty obvious that when you're stirring or shaking a drink, you're blending its ingredients. Both shaking and stirring do that job perfectly well. What distinguishes stirred from shaken drinks, though, is texture. Stirred drinks have a silky texture, whereas shaken drinks have a somewhat foamy texture.

Now, when you think of the ingredients in a cocktail, most likely you focus on the base liquor, any liqueurs or other modifiers, fruit juice, bitters, and so on. But chances are you'll overlook one essential ingredient: water. Few recipes in this book call for water, so how does it get there? By mixing with ice.

What's more, the cocktail's potent flavors often come into balance with the addition of this small amount of water, which also helps to cool the burn of alcohol on the palate.

WHEN SHOULD I STIR AND WHEN SHOULD I SHAKE?

Of the two methods for mixing drinks—shaking and stirring—shaking is a more efficient way to chill and dilute a drink. Simply, this is because the ice rattles around violently in the shaker and therefore breaks down more quickly, releasing its water into the drink. However, what the ice also does is agitate the drink, causing it to foam up and form a bubbly texture. This means that shaking is not always the proper method for making a cocktail.

So, when is it best to shake and when is it best to stir? Here's the rule of thumb:

- Shake any drink that contains juice, dairy, or eggs. These ingredients already have a thicker texture than any of the booze in the shaker, and therefore they generally look better in a glass and have a better texture when they're foamy. Think of how satisfying whipped cream and meringue taste and feel.

- Stir any drink that is made from just spirits—including the Boulevardier, Manhattan, Sazerac, Rob Roy, or most variations on the Brooklyn.

HOW TO STIR A COCKTAIL

Stirring is an easy skill to master, though doing it correctly requires a special technique and a bar spoon.

WHAT YOU'LL NEED:

- A mixing glass
- The ingredients for your drink
- Ice
- A bar spoon

WHAT YOU'LL DO:

1. Chill both your mixing glass and your serving glass. Store them for at least 30 minutes in the freezer or at least an hour in the fridge. Alternatively, you can fill them with a mix of ice and water and set aside for 5 minutes. If you use a glass at room temperature, the glass will warm its contents and dilute the cocktail too quickly. A cold glass helps chill the drink and slows down dilution.

2. Dump the ice water, if using, from the mixing glass.

3. Add cocktail ingredients to the empty mixing glass, starting with the least expensive and ending with the base spirit. This way, if you make a mistake while measuring and you need to dump it out and start over, you're not wasting the good stuff. Start with any fruit juice the recipe calls for, then add liqueurs or vermouths or other modifying liquors, and finally add your base spirit.

4. Add enough cracked ice to fill the mixing glass about ⅔ full. Here's the best way to crack the ice: Wash your hands well, take a standard cube in one hand, and then whack it with the back of the bowl of your bar spoon to crack it into smaller pieces.

5. Take your spoon between your thumb and your first two fingers of your dominant hand. The shaft of the spoon should be between your index and middle finger. Insert the spoon into the glass until the bowl of the spoon touches the bottom.

6. Keeping your arm and fingers still, use your wrist to turn the spoon in the glass. The spoon, you'll find, will spin about in your fingers on its own axis. Use your index finger to pull the spoon toward you (from the 12 o'clock position to the six o'clock) and your middle finger to push it away. The ice and liquid will move about the glass. After you've had some practice with this, you'll find it's pretty easy to move the spoon up and down in the glass while you're stirring. You should stir it this way because it helps to agitate the drink. As you get really good at this technique, you can even close your eyes and enjoy the sensation of the spoon spinning in your hand.

7. Stir for about 25–30 seconds. If you want to be scientific about this, insert a digital thermometer into the glass. If the temperature reads about 20°F (about −7°C), you're done. If not, keep stirring.

8. Dump the ice water, if using, from the serving glass. Strain the stirred cocktail into the chilled serving glass, garnish, and serve.

HOW TO SHAKE A COCKTAIL

Go into any decent cocktail bar and watch the bartenders. You'll soon see that each bartender has a unique style for using the cocktail shaker. Some shake up and down; some shake back and forth; and others seem to be violently rocking the shaker. It might all seem a bit crazy, but I promise that shaking is a pretty easy technique to master if you follow the steps I outline here. And unlike stirring, shaking allows you to express personal style and wit, which are always fun guests at a cocktail party.

WHAT YOU'LL NEED:
- Cocktail shaker
- The ingredients for your cocktail
- Ice

If you're using a Boston shaker, you might have two questions about it: First, how do I close it so that it doesn't leak? Second, how do I open the damn thing to get to my drink? Both predicaments have simple solutions, described in the following step-by-step instructions.

WHAT YOU'LL DO:

1. Chill your serving glass. You can store it for at least 15 minutes in the freezer or 30 minutes in the fridge, or you can fill it with a mix of ice and water and set aside for 5 minutes.

2. Measure and pour your ingredients into the mixing glass without ice. Use the same technique I mentioned in the stirring section, where you add ingredients in the order of cheapest to most expensive. (First juice, then liqueurs or vermouth, and finally the base spirit.)

3. Add two large ice cubes. (I like the Tovolo King Cube Ice Tray molds for this, which make large cubes of 2 inches per side.) Add a couple of smaller (1-inch) cubes as well.

4. To close the shaker so that it doesn't leak when you're shaking, you need to ensure that you have a tight seal. Place the empty metal mixing tin over the top of the glass at a slight angle. Using the heel of your hand, tap sharply against the base of the tin. You don't need to hit the tin hard, just firmly. If you've sealed the shaker properly, you should be able to pick up the entire contraption from your counter or table just by lifting the tin. If you lift the tin and the glass stays put, you don't have a seal.

5. Hold the glass away from your guests, in your dominant hand over your shoulder. If anything leaks from the shaker, it will leak away from your guests and behind you (instead of spraying your guests in the face).

6. Shake vigorously for at least 15 seconds. You want to break up the ice and mix everything thoroughly. A short, wimpy shake will

not achieve this. You don't need to go crazy, though. You should hear the ice rattling around in the shaker, striking the sides, top, and bottom.

7. To break the seal when you're done shaking, hold the shaker in your nondominant hand and look at it carefully. What you'll see is that the tin and glass are in a curved shape, like a banana. On the inner part of the curve, the tin and glass are snuggled up tightly together. On the outer part of the curve, there's a wider gap between them. What you're looking for is the spot where the two just start to separate. This is where you'll aim to hit the thing with the heel of your dominant hand to break it apart. Again, you don't need to hit it hard, just firmly, right where the gap is starting to form.

8. Remove the mixing glass from the tin and set aside, leaving the cocktail and ice in the tin. Then dump ice water (if using) from the serving glass. Strain the shaken cocktail into serving glass. Garnish and drink it down.

HOW TO STRAIN A COCKTAIL

Traditionally, a julep strainer is used when straining a cocktail from a mixing glass, and a Hawthorne is used when straining from a mixing tin. The reason is simple: The julep strainer fits a mixing glass a little better than a Hawthorne does, and the Hawthorne's a better fit than a julep when using a tin. Stick to this tradition and you're less likely to make a mess when pouring.

HOW TO STRAIN USING A JULEP STRAINER

WHAT YOU'LL NEED:
- Julep strainer
- Mixing glass full of cocktail and ice
- Chilled serving glass

1. Place the julep strainer in the mixing glass, with the bowl of the strainer "cupping" the ice, like a bowl placed upside down.

2. Grab the mixing glass near its rim, using your dominant hand. Using your index finger, hold the strainer against the ice. Lift the mixing glass, tilt it over the serving glass, and pour.

HOW TO STRAIN USING A HAWTHORNE STRAINER

WHAT YOU'LL NEED:
- Hawthorne strainer
- Mixing tin full of cocktail
- Chilled serving glass

WHAT YOU'LL DO:

1. Place the Hawthorne strainer atop the mixing tin, using the strainer's tabs to keep it from falling into the tin.

2. Grasp the tin near the top, using your dominant hand. Use your index finger or first two fingers to hold the strainer in place.

3. Using your fingers, slide the strainer forward against the tin so that no gap remains between the front rim of the strainer and the lip of the tin. This helps keep tiny shards of ice, bits of fruit, and muddled leaves inside the tin and out of the drink.

4. Lift the mixing tin, holding the strainer in place with one or two fingers. Tilt it over the serving glass, and pour.

5. When nearly all the cocktail is in the glass, snap your wrist once toward the glass and again away from it, using the shaking motion to remove the last few drops of cocktail from the shaker tin.

ADDING SODA

The traditional instructions for mixing highballs such as the Morning Glory Cocktail (page 117) say to shake the main ingredients together, strain into a glass, and then top with soda water. In most cases, this leaves you with a dense cocktail at the bottom of the glass and a bunch of soda water floating on top. Gross.

There's a better way, and I learned it from Jeffrey Morgenthaler's *The Bar Book*. Shake the main ingredients and then add the fizzy stuff to the shaker before you strain. Makes sense: The act of straining will agitate the drink enough to mix the ingredients a bit, and the heavier alcohol will essentially be poured over the soda, creating a much more even mix.

WHEN SHOULD I DOUBLE STRAIN?

Some cocktails call for an extra step, a special bit of finesse to make them smooth and pretty. When you're straining a cocktail that contains fruit, mint, or muddled ginger, it's easy when straining to let little bits of fruit pulp or muddled leaves slip through a Hawthorne strainer, muddy up your cocktail, and provide an unpleasant texture.

Using a fine mesh strainer, such as a handheld tea strainer, allows you to filter out those bits of detritus and present a crisp and perfectly clear cocktail.

WHAT YOU'LL NEED:

- Mixing tin full of cocktail
- Hawthorne strainer
- Fine mesh strainer
- Chilled serving glass

WHAT YOU'LL DO:

1. Strain the drink with a Hawthorne strainer as instructed previously, but use your nondominant hand to hold a mesh strainer above the serving glass.

2. Strain the cocktail from the Hawthorne strainer through the mesh strainer and into the glass.

HOW TO MAKE A CITRUS TWIST

A twist of citrus peel (also called a citrus twist) provides more than just an attractive grace note atop a cocktail. When made deftly, a fresh piece of fruit imparts something very important to the finish of a good cocktail: citrus oil.

The oil is there to boost the aroma of the drink. If you engage all your senses as you go in for that first sip, you'll notice a blast of fresh citrus drifting off the glass.

To make a twist, start with a fresh lemon or orange, preferably organic. (Pesticides are not a welcome cocktail ingredient. Neither is wax, which often coats even organic fruit. One way to remove the wax, if it concerns you, is to flash-boil each piece right before using, and then scrub off the wax with a vegetable brush.)

You'll also need a paring knife or vegetable peeler.

WHAT YOU'LL DO:

1. Hold the fruit in your nondominant hand with your thumb near the top pole (where the stem attached to the fruit) and your pinky supporting the bottom point.

2. Take the knife and cut toward you, slowly, through the peel. Be careful not to cut too deeply into the pith, which is bitter and will make your drink taste the same way. Don't worry about cutting an attractive shape; just cut an elongated oval.

3. Take the peel in both hands, between the thumb and forefinger of each hand. Twist and squeeze it over the glass, peel side down, to express the citrus oil onto the surface of the drink.

4. Rub the peel around the rim of the glass to provide a little extra flavor. Either discard the twist or drop it into the drink, depending on what the recipe calls for.

HOW TO MUDDLE MINT OR OTHER HERBS

Look closely at a mint leaf. You should see little veins running through it. Those veins contain chlorophyll, and as it turns out, chlorophyll is bitter. Don't make a rookie mistake and bash the crap out of your mint. You'll just release the bitter chlorophyll into your julep. No one wants that.

You can buy a muddler if you want to, though a wooden spoon or the handle of a rolling pin will do in a pinch. If you do buy a wooden muddler, be careful what you buy. You want a muddler that has not been varnished or lacquered. The varnish on a muddler will eventually wear off, and you do not want that in your drink.

Muddlers made of stainless steel, or those with a plastic or hard-rubber muddling base, will work, too. But avoid the type with teeth on the end; they're great for muddling the juice and oils from fruit, but they'll shred the leaves of mint and other herbs.

WHAT YOU'LL DO:

1. Choose a sturdy mixing glass, a pint glass, or a shaker tin. If you choose a thin-walled glass, you risk breaking or chipping the glass with your muddler.

2. Place the leaves into the bottom of the glass. Add sugar or lemon wedges or whatever the recipe requires.

3. Press down with the muddler lightly on the leaves and the other ingredients that need muddling. Twist gently, rocking the muddler without shredding the leaves. If there's also fruit in the glass, you should see juice squirting out from the flesh.

4. When your kitchen smells like freshly pressed herb, you're done. Your mint should look largely intact and a little damp, not shredded into a bajillion pieces. You don't want your mint to go all the way to the pulverized stage—you just want to release its minty aromas!

HOW TO MAKE EGGS FOAM

If you want to make a Morning Glory Fizz (page 118), you're gonna need to froth up some egg whites. They'll add a silky, foamy texture to the drink.

You'll use a technique that bartenders call a *dry shake*. The idea of the dry shake is to emulsify the egg whites into the drink, without ice, to build a thicker, more stable foam structure. You then shake again, with ice, to dilute and chill and further blend the drink.

HERE'S HOW YOU DO IT:
1. Add egg whites and liquor-type ingredients to a mixing glass, as you would normally when shaking a cocktail. But don't add the ice.

2. Place shaker tin standing right side up, with the open end facing the ceiling. Pour the contents of mixing glass into the shaker tin, and then place the top of the mixing glass into the top of the tin— dead center, rather than at an angle.

3. Smack the glass with your hand to seal the shaker.

4. Shake, shake, shake.

5. Separate the glass from the tin, add ice, and seal as normal—that is, at a slight angle. Shake again.

6. Strain and sip!

CITRUS: CONVENTIONAL VS. ORGANIC

Unless you're lucky enough to live in a climate suitable for growing citrus, you'll probably need to buy your limes and lemons at a grocery store. There's not much to think about when buying citrus, except for this . . .

Organic or conventional? Conventional citrus looks great but it's been sprayed with pesticides and fungicides and . . . yuck. If you're simply juicing the citrus, this might not be a problem for you. Citrus is generally thick-skinned enough that sprays don't penetrate into the fruit. So just rinse the fruit briefly before cutting it so that your knife doesn't drag the pesticide/fungicide residue across the interior of the fruit.

If you're going to be using the zest, though, you might think about buying organic, so you can avoid drinking these residues. Organic fruit does, in my experience, go bad more quickly than conventional. Just make sure you don't overbuy, or you'll have moldy fruit to discard.

JUICING CITRUS IN A HINGE-STYLE SQUEEZER

When using a hinge-style squeezer, there are a few ways to make the job easier and more efficient. First, cut off both ends. Hand squeezers hate them, and besides, how much juice do the ends hold? None.

Second, turn the citrus over so that the cut side (the fruit flesh) rests against the inner cup. When you squeeze, you'll be turning the rind basically inside out. Not only does this make for more efficient juicing, but it also directs the juice where it needs to go, which is through the perforations in the cup and into your juice receptacle. If you squeeze the citrus half the other way, the juice jets up out of the squeezer and onto your face, hands, shirt, and work surface.

THE FLAVOR RINSE

The purpose of the rinse is to impart the taste of a strongly flavored ingredient into a cocktail, but without that ingredient overpowering the rest of the drink.

The Sazerac is probably the best-known cocktail to feature a rinse, with its traditional wash of absinthe (or pastis, in the decades before absinthe's return to the United States). In the case of the Sazerac, the absinthe provides a hint of anise flavor, which complements the rye whiskey and enhances similar spicy notes in the Peychaud's Bitters.

Writing in *Esquire* magazine, David Wondrich suggests other uses for the cocktail rinse. One of his ideas that I've tried and now love is a rinse of single malt Scotch in a Manhattan cocktail.

WHAT YOU'LL NEED:

- Rinse ingredient (absinthe, Scotch, liqueur, etc.)
- Glass

WHAT YOU'LL DO:

1. Pour about ¼ ounce of your rinse ingredient into the glass.

2. Swirl the glass quickly so the rinse splashes around the sides of the glass.

3. Tip the glass so that the rinse reaches the rim of the glass, and then slowly turn it so the rinse coats the interior side of the glass.

4. Discard excess rinse, either down the sink or down your throat. Fill rinsed glass with cocktail and serve.

HOW TO CREATE A COCKTAIL

Vancouver's Lauren Mote is a rising star in the bar scene, a bar manager at Uva Wine & Cocktail Bar in Downtown Vancouver, and one of the bitters makers behind Bittered Sling. Lauren was named bartender of the year by both the Vancouver Magazine Restaurant Awards and Diageo World Class Canada, so I knew that when I wanted someone to give me a glimpse into Vancouver's cocktail scene, she was the person to talk to.

Lauren told me, "As a creative professional, I am inspired by all kinds of things, and that's the beginning of my process. I used to loosely tell those inquiring that 'I'm inspired by nouns: people, places, and things' . . . I'll start with the theme, and choose a classic design that fits the bill. From there, I'll develop the story and *mise en place,* and then start to move the ingredients around until I hit the jackpot. It doesn't take long to *make* a cocktail; it's the story and the name that takes the most time—that's the intellectual part."

For the drink she contributed to this book, Lauren saw an opportunity to tell the history of Canada through a cocktail, and that's one of the recurring themes of this book: whiskey as history in a glass.

I asked Lauren to describe how she picks a base spirit for her original cocktails, and then how she crafts the rest of the drink to incorporate and highlight the base and the other ingredients. "The base whisky has to do two things," she told me. "One, carry the story and *fit* the story of the cocktail. And, two, make a positive contribution to the remaining ingredients in the cocktail. I choose other ingredients based on their density for the cocktail, and their relevance for the cocktail's story."

Now, let's see how this all plays out in the following cocktail that she contributed.

THE ACADIEN

This cocktail design celebrates two of Canada's topographical areas, the Canadian Shield and the Appalachian Mountains (Central and Eastern Canada). With wonderful notes of maple, rye, fruit, and herbaceous roots, The Acadien pulls inspiration directly from the earliest French settlers in the maritime/Quebec regions.

INGREDIENTS

1½ ounces Canadian Club 100% Rye Whisky

½ ounce Sortilège Canadian Whisky and Maple Syrup Liqueur

½ ounce Amontillado sherry

¼ ounce Giffard Abricot du Roussillon liqueur

3 dashes Bittered Sling Cascade Celery Bitters

Lemon peel

Cinnamon stick, for garnish

Thyme sprig, for garnish

Lemon cheek, for garnish

PROCEDURE

1. Stir all liquid ingredients together and pour over a large cube in an old-fashioned glass.

2. Squeeze the lemon peel over the surface of the glass, rub the rim with the peel, and discard the peel.

3. Finish the cocktail with a garnish of thin cinnamon stick and flowering thyme sprig threaded through a lemon cheek.

NOTE

To cut a lemon cheek, first cut the end off a lemon. It can be the stem end (the end with the dimple) or the other end. Set the lemon on the cut end to keep it secure on the board. Holding the knife perpendicular to the board, cut about ½ an inch of the fruit off. This is the cheek.

Chapter 4

HISTORIC WHISKEY COCKTAILS

Now that I've walked you briefly through the histories and stories of each major style of whiskey, it's time to tell the stories of many famous (and not so famous) whiskey cocktails. I'll work through this in roughly chronological order, from the first whiskey drinks anyone enjoyed up through the modern classics of the last 15 years. I'll even throw in a few new creations, which I hope you'll enjoy. Unlike most history, however, this is cocktail history, which means you can drink it as you read it. Enjoy!

CHERRY BOUNCE
OR, A REMINDER OF SUMMER IN DEEP DECEMBER

In 1784, after helping secure American independence but before taking the presidency, George Washington set out on a journey into the frontier, hoping to find a navigable waterway from the Potomac River to the Ohio River Valley.

In his journals, he discussed his provisioning. For the purpose of this book we're not interested in the notes about his tent poles, horseshoes, or bedding. But we are interested in his potables (forgive the strange spelling, capitalization, and use of punctuation—they're George's, not mine).

> Note.—in my equipage Trunk and the Canteens—were Madeira and Port Wine—Cherry Bounce—Oyl, Mustard—Vinegar—and Spices of all sorts—Tea and sugar in the camp kettles . . .

In her own papers, his wife Martha left records of her bounce recipe. So, we have some idea about this Cherry Bounce that he must have been drinking on this journey.

Bounce is one of the easiest things you can do with a rich brown spirit, such as whiskey, rum, or brandy. You simply pour it into a half-gallon jar and add a bunch of ripe cherries. Leave the fruit in the spirit long enough, and you'll find that the spirit picks up all the flavor and color of the rich, red cherries.

INGREDIENTS

There's no formal recipe here. Use a pound of cherries and a single 750-ml bottle of bourbon, nothing fancy.

NOTE

The timing is pretty good for this recipe. In most of North America, cherries hit farmer's markets in July and August. Three months after July is October. Two months after October is December. Christmas is in December. Put up your cherries in July, and you'll have a nice reminder of summer in the heart of winter.

PROCEDURE

1. Stem the cherries, but don't bother pitting them. Pierce them with a knife to give the bourbon an entryway into the flesh of the fruit. Add two cups of sugar or more to taste. A couple sticks of cinnamon and some grated nutmeg would spice it up and be authentic to Martha's recipe.

2. Shake everything up so the sugar starts to dissolve and store in a dark place. Shake it every few days at first, but then you can leave it alone for three months and let the magic happen.

3. After three months, strain off the cherries, pressing them to squeeze out the bourbon-soaked juice. The cherries will probably be gray and dead-looking, so discard them. At this point, you can store the bounce for two more months.

STONE FENCE

One of the oldest drinks detailed in this book, the Stone Fence, originated in the Colonial era. It's a simple drink; in its original form, it consisted of rum and hard cider. The drink is versatile, though, and you can mix it with anything that is rich and hearty: applejack, other brandies, or rye whiskey.

Look for a dry hard cider, nothing too sweet. A store specializing in beer should have some good options. Of course, if you make your own cider, just use that. If you really want to be Colonial-authentic, a young whiskey or even a white whiskey would work well here.

INGREDIENTS

2 ounces rye or bourbon whiskey

Hard cider

PROCEDURE

1. In a pint glass, place two large ice cubes. Add whiskey and cider and stir.

TODDY

At the beginning of the toddy, drinkers took the brew hot in the winter and cold (or, more likely, room temperature) in the summer. I can't think of anyone who takes a room-temperature toddy these days. If you want watered-down whiskey on a hot day, have an icy-cold highball. No one with sense will blame you, and a person of very good sense will probably join you. But a highball isn't a cold toddy; it's its own thing.

In his book *Imbibe!* David Wondrich points out that as American history progressed, so did America's choice of spirit for the toddy, moving from rum to brandy, bourbon, and rye. But around the time that Jerry Thomas wrote his pivotal cocktail book, *Bartender's Guide,* in the 1870s, Americans had begun drinking it with single malt Scotch, not the blended Scotch, which wasn't yet common in the States.

In fact, any spirit made in a pot still, as single malts are, is excellent in a toddy. The richness and texture of a pot-stilled spirit are somehow enhanced by the addition of hot water and a good brown sugar, such as demerara. Bourbon and rye will work, but for the best hot toddy, use single malt Scotch (really peaty varieties, such as Lagavulin, are fantastic) or pure pot-still Irish whiskey, such as Redbreast, which is spectacular in a hot toddy.

INGREDIENTS

3–4 ounces boiling water, more to warm cup

1 teaspoon sugar

2 ounces whiskey of choice

PROCEDURE

1. Fill a mug with boiling water; let it sit to warm up for a few minutes, and discard the water.

2. Add sugar to the empty mug, and then add 3–4 ounces boiling water. Allow sugar time to dissolve.

3. Add whiskey and stir to combine.

WHISKEY SLING

Arising shortly after the toddy, in the 18th century, the sling was originally just a toddy topped with grated nutmeg. As the ice trade took off in the early 19th century, though, the sling increasingly became an iced drink that consisted of spirit, sugar, water, ice, and nutmeg. In its original definition, a *cocktail* was also called a bittered sling. And sure enough, if you remove the nutmeg and add bitters, you have something that most people would recognize as an old-fashioned.

For the toddy, I suggest single malt Scotch or Irish whiskey. But you can use just about anything for the sling. Rye and bourbon work just as well in an iced sling as they do in an old-fashioned, which is to say excellently well.

INGREDIENTS

2 ounces whiskey of your choice

½ teaspoon superfine sugar

¼ ounce water

Nutmeg, for garnish

PROCEDURE

1. In a rocks glass, add whiskey, sugar, and water, and stir well to combine and dissolve sugar.

2. Add three ice cubes and stir well.

3. Grate nutmeg over the top of the drink.

—◦• THE ICEMAN COMETH •◦—

Before the invention of modern refrigeration, having ice around to preserve food and other perishables (or to chill down a drink) was a luxury. Noblemen and royalty in Europe would collect ice and snow in the winter and store them in private ice houses for the purpose of chilling drinks and preserving perishables. But this practice didn't trickle down to the general population until the 1700s.

An 18th-century ice vendor usually served his own local community, cutting blocks of lake ice in the winter and then packing them tightly together in ice houses, insulated with straw or sawdust. Ice wagons would pick up the ice and deliver it into town, where customers would store it in an icebox in the home or business. The icebox was a sort of proto-refrigerator, an insulated box that would keep the cold generated by the ice in the box, to preserve food.

In the early days of the ice trade, the business was purely local. All that changed in 1805 when Frederic Tudor joined the trade. He envisioned being able to earn great wealth from the trade, and in that year, he shipped a brig full of ice to Martinique. Unfortunately, the heat of the voyage melted the ice and the trip was a failure.

Undiscouraged, Tudor worked on the problem. He devised ways to pack the ice in more tightly and surround it with sawdust to insulate it and keep it . . . well . . . ice cold. By 1820, Tudor was servicing the American South (including New Orleans); by 1833, his trade reached Calcutta; and the following year, he shipped ice to Rio de Janeiro. By 1856, Tudor was shipping 146,000 tons of ice; and by 1880, that number had skyrocketed to 890,000 tons.

American cities, especially on the coasts, bought a lot of the ice that was cut and shipped by Tudor and his competitors. This ever-growing trade quickly brought ice into the realm of the bartender, where it rapidly became ubiquitous in such drinks as the whiskey sling and the julep.

MINT JULEP

The mint julep is one of the oldest existing beverages, with roots in Persia reaching back over one thousand years ago. The word *julep* arises from the Persian *golâb*, "rosewater," and it initially described a drink of sugar, some sort of medicinal herb or flower, and water. For the first eight or so centuries of its life, this was purely a medicinal drink—an herbal tonic sweetened with sugar to make it more palatable. As early as 1714, physicians were prescribing juleps made with brandy or wine for various ailments. A British physician, Thomas Fuller, offered several julep recipes in a book published that year. Most contain no alcohol, but some have wine or brandy.

A reference to a "julep" served as a beverage, not as a medicine, appears in a 1763 burlesque poem, *Don Coblero: or, The Mock Baron*:

> A bowl was brought of best French brandy,
> 'Twas fit for Baron, Count, or Grandee;
> The apparatus thus before 'em,
> In neatest order and decorum;
> The Baron strokes his chin or dewlap,
> Then drinks a health of cordial julep;

Crafty Southerners decided—no one's quite sure when, but sometime in the 1700s is likely—to spike the julep with booze to make it even more palatable. That booze, however, was not bourbon or even whiskey that we're used to drinking in the julep today. Julep makers used the stuff they already had on hand, namely wine, rum, genever, and, most notably, cognac.

With an origin in the 18th century, the boozy julep came along before American whiskey was widely available. And even when American whiskey was more available, the julep had become a drink of the genteel South, and in that time, gentlemen drank brandy and rum, not brash American whiskey.

The man who made juleps famous wasn't a Southerner at all, but a fellow from Massachusetts who moved just a bit south in 1813 to take a job at New York's City Hotel. At the time, it was the country's most famous hotel. Within a couple of years of arriving, Orsamus Willard became its bartender. In 1817, a traveling Virginian introduced Willard to the joys of the iced julep. With the ice trade taking off, it was suddenly easy to get ice. Willard was the most popular bartender at the most famous hotel in the country; it didn't take long for his customers to spread word about his wondrous juleps.

Willard, though, was probably still fixing brandy juleps. Bourbon finally took over the drink after the American Civil War, when, for whatever reason, drinkers' tastes changed to prefer American whiskey over French brandy. Thus the drink as we now know it came into being.

It's easy to make one at home. You'll need a lot of crushed ice for this; use a blender to make the job easier. Use a julep cup, if you can find one. With the rise of the craft cocktail movement, such items are far more available than they were when I started into this hobby/obsession over a decade ago. The cup will frost up beautifully and keep the drink icy cold. Wrap a linen towel around it to protect your hand, if you're easily frostbitten.

INGREDIENTS

8 mint leaves (and 1 mint sprig for garnish)

1 teaspoon simple syrup

3 ounces high-proof bourbon or rye whiskey

PROCEDURE

1. Add mint and simple syrup to a julep cup or rocks glass. Take a muddler and swab the mint around inside the cup to coat the cup in minty joy.

2. (Optional) Conversely, you can omit the mint and simple syrup and use 1 teaspoon Mint Syrup (page 211) instead.

3. Add whiskey and stir.

4. Add crushed ice to the top of the cup and stir. The ice will melt and sink below the top of the cup. Add more ice until it mounds over the top.

5. Insert a mint sprig into the ice. Insert a straw next to the mint, so that as you drink the julep, you smell the mint.

WHISKEY COBBLER

The cobbler is one of the oldest drinks in a bartender's arsenal, and once upon a time, it was the most popular drink in the United States. It's fallen from popularity somehow, and other writers (David Wondrich, in his *Imbibe!*, for example) have tried to resurrect it. I wish more people would try the cobbler. I had a sherry cobbler in Boston while promoting my first book, and I fell in love.

The sherry cobbler, in fact, is the oldest version of the drink, arising in the 1830s. It's a refreshing tipple—low in alcohol, icier than a julep, and very mildly fruity. The whiskey variation is, of course, a stronger, more bracing drink. But sometimes that's what you want.

INGREDIENTS

4 ounces rye whiskey (high-proof, like Rittenhouse)

1 tablespoon simple syrup

3 orange slices

Berries (optional; ideally, fresh, local, and seasonal—so if you're making this in winter, I wouldn't bother)

PROCEDURE

1. Crack a whole lot of ice. You want something like little pebbles. Best bet: Fill a gallon-sized zipper bag with ice, place a towel over it, and wallop it with a rolling pin, meat mallet, or saucepan.

2. Fill a shaker with the cracked ice, as much as you can fit. Add the whiskey, simple syrup, and orange slices.

3. Shake vigorously to combine.

4. Pour unstrained into a collins glass. Add more ice if you want and stir.

5. Garnish with berries, if using.

WHISKEY SMASH

The Brandy Smash dates to about the 1830s, and gave rise later to versions starring gin and whiskey. It owes a lot to the julep, from which it descended. But whereas a julep is a sipping cocktail, the Smash is a bracer, meant to be tossed back quickly.

This version was popularized by Dale DeGroff, when he worked at the Rainbow Room atop 30 Rockefeller Plaza in Manhattan. DeGroff's version differs from the classic mainly by the addition of lemon to the drink. His method, of smashing pieces of lemon into the mixing glass, expresses both the juice and the oils in the peel, resulting in a more complex drink.

DeGroff has stated that he prefers the Smash to the julep, and maybe you will, too. Try them both and see!

INGREDIENTS

½ lemon, quartered

5 large mint leaves

¾ ounce simple syrup

2 ounces bourbon (Maker's Mark Cask Strength is fantastic in this—use it if you can; 12 Year Old Elijah Craig is good, too)

Mint sprigs, for garnish

PROCEDURE

1. In a cocktail shaker, add lemon wedges and mint. Take a muddler and smash gently, just to express the juices and oils from the lemon.

2. Add simple syrup, bourbon, and ice. Shake well to chill and combine.

3. Strain into an ice-filled rocks glass. Add garnish.

WHISKEY CRUSTA

Much like the cobbler, the Crusta doesn't get much love nowadays, and I'd like to see that change. It's a good drink with a fun presentation and a bit of interesting history. According to David Wondrich, the Crusta arose in New Orleans around 1850. It owes its basic form to the original cocktail—booze, bitters, sugar, and water—adding one element that sets it apart: citrus juice. The Crusta was among the first cocktails to include citrus, which is surprising given how ubiquitous it is in drinks today.

INGREDIENTS

1 lemon, for peel and juice

2 ounces bourbon whiskey

1 teaspoon superfine sugar, plus more for rim

1 teaspoon simple syrup

½ teaspoon orange curaçao

2 dashes Angostura bitters

PROCEDURE

1. Using a vegetable peeler, cut around the equator of a lemon, removing about half the peel. Set aside.

2. Juice 1 teaspoon of the lemon.

3. Take a small wine glass (about 3–4 ounces in capacity), dip the rim in lemon juice, and then dip the rim again in superfine sugar.

4. Place the lemon peel in the glass so it emerges over the edge of the glass.

5. In a mixing glass, add ice until about ⅔ full, and then add remaining ingredients.

6. Strain the cocktail into the prepared glass.

WHISKEY SOUR

Though quite a few whiskey cocktails predate the American Civil War, I can think of only three that are still popular today: the mint julep, the old-fashioned, and the whiskey sour, the last of which arose around 1850. The sour is a simple drink: whiskey, lemon juice, and sugar. It gave rise to many of the most popular drinks in history. The margarita, for example, is tequila, lime, and triple sec. The daiquiri swaps out the tequila for rum and uses sugar as the sweetener. The sidecar marries cognac with lemon and triple sec.

I like my whiskey sours sour, so I don't use much sugar. Adjust this to your own preference. Historically, the sour was a bourbon drink, but if you prefer rye or Irish or Canadian or even Scotch, go for it.

INGREDIENTS

2 ounces bourbon whiskey

½ ounce lemon juice

1 teaspoon sugar

Lemon peel, for garnish

PROCEDURE

1. Add whiskey, lemon juice, and sugar to a shaker filled ⅔ with ice.

2. Shake well to dissolve sugar and chill the drink.

3. Strain into a chilled cocktail glass.

4. Squeeze the lemon peel over the surface of the glass, rub the rim with the peel, and drop the peel into the glass.

PRESCRIPTION JULEP

Harper's Magazine bills itself as the oldest general-interest magazine in America. In 1857 it was busy publishing, among other things, the serialization of Charles Dickens's *Little Dorrit.* Also appearing in the magazine was a humorous travelogue called "A Winter in the South," written and illustrated by David Hunter Strother. He spins a yarn about a traveler who reads the political news every day and therefore suffers from a dyspeptic stomach. He consults a physician, who gives him a beverage "prescription," which the traveler quaffs daily, and thus recovers his "health and jollity." I suspect that you, too, will feel hale and jolly after drinking one of these.

For the "strong cognac" in the recipe, you want something stronger than the 80 proof stuff that's so widely available. I suggest Louis Royer Force 53, bottled at 106 proof. If you can't find that, use Pierre Ferrand 1840, bottled at 90 proof. For the rye, anything will suffice.

INGREDIENTS

½ ounce simple syrup

2 sprigs mint, plus more for garnish

2 ounces strong cognac (I suggest Louis Royer Force 53)

½ ounce rye whiskey

¼ ounce Jamaican rum, to float on top (optional; I suggest Appleton or Smith & Cross)

PROCEDURE

1. Add simple syrup and mint to a julep cup or rocks glass. Muddle the mint lightly to release its oils.

2. Add cognac and rye and stir to combine.

3. Fill glass with crushed ice and stir to chill until the cup or glass begins to frost. Add more ice as needed, until it mounds over the top.

4. Using the back of a bar spoon, gently float the Jamaican rum atop ice (if using).

5. Garnish with a sprig of mint and serve with a straw.

1860–1899

THE FIRST GOLDEN AGE
OF THE COCKTAIL

WHISKEY COCKTAIL

Now we come back around to the true cocktail. The first known definition of the cocktail described it as spirits of any kind, plus sugar, water, and bitters. Though this concept clearly dates from the early 1800s and therefore could have appeared in the previous section of this book, I place the whiskey cocktail here, because it's sort of the ur-cocktail for many of the recipes that follow. This recipe, from Jerry Thomas's 1862 book *Bartender's Guide,* fits the bill perfectly. I'm including it here mostly as a historic curiosity, though feel free to test it out and see how you like it.

You'll note it's essentially an Old-Fashioned (pages 124–125) but offered up without ice in the serving glass. (The Sazerac—pages 136–137—borrows this service style exactly.) In Thomas's book, this recipe was a template that called for brandy, genever, or whiskey. The genever version is especially good, but—wait, isn't this a whiskey book?

INGREDIENTS

2 ounces bourbon or rye whiskey

1 teaspoon simple or gomme syrup

2 dashes Angostura bitters

Lemon peel, for garnish

PROCEDURE

1. In a mixing glass ⅔ full of ice, pour bourbon, simple syrup, and bitters.

2. Stir at least 30 seconds, or until drink is cold and diluted.

3. Strain into a chilled rocks glass.

4. Squeeze the lemon peel over the surface of the glass, rub the rim with the peel, and drop the peel into the glass.

FANCY WHISKEY COCKTAIL

What makes this fancy? Just a splash of orange liqueur and the serving vessel, that's what. This recipe is mainly in this book as a historic curiosity, but it's still a satisfying drink. There are worse ways to study history than by drinking it.

INGREDIENTS

2 ounces bourbon or rye whiskey

1 teaspoon simple or gomme syrup

2 dashes Angostura bitters

¼ ounce Grand Marnier

Lemon peel, for garnish

PROCEDURE

1. In a mixing glass ⅔ full of ice, pour bourbon, simple syrup, bitters, and Grand Marnier.

2. Stir at least 30 seconds, or until drink is cold and diluted.

3. Strain into a chilled red wine glass.

4. Squeeze the lemon peel over the surface of the glass, rub the rim with the peel, and drop the peel into the glass.

IMPROVED WHISKEY COCKTAIL

What makes this improved? For one, the Grand Marnier from the Fancy Whiskey Cocktail is gone, replaced by maraschino liqueur. But the most important thing is the addition of absinthe, which provides a subtle anise flavor. I prefer rye over bourbon for this.

INGREDIENTS

2 ounces rye whiskey

1 teaspoon simple or gomme syrup

2 dashes Angostura bitters

¼ ounce maraschino liqueur

1 dash absinthe

Lemon peel, for garnish

PROCEDURE

1. In a mixing glass ⅔ full of ice, pour whiskey, simple syrup, bitters, maraschino liqueur, and absinthe.

2. Stir at least 30 seconds, or until drink is cold and diluted.

3. Strain into a chilled red wine glass.

4. Squeeze the lemon peel over the surface of the glass, rub the rim with the peel, and drop the peel into the glass.

MORNING GLORY COCKTAIL

Whenever you see phrases like *morning glory*, *eye opener*, or *corpse reviver* in the name of a drink, it's safe to assume these are hair-of-the-dog drinks—hangover helpers. In 19th-century America, cocktails weren't just for dinner—they were for breakfast, lunch, and midday snacks as well. The history of the cocktail, in fact, is intricately interwoven with hangover cures, as the booze historian David Wondrich points out in his book *Imbibe!* Both this cocktail and the Morning Glory Fizz (page 118) are prime examples.

Though I'm neither your doctor nor your priest, I don't suggest hair-of-the-dog drinks as a daily tipple. However, both Morning Glory drinks noted in this book would make fantastic brunch drinks.

INGREDIENTS

1 ounce cognac

1 ounce rye whiskey

¼ teaspoon simple syrup

2 dashes Cointreau

2 dashes Angostura bitters

1 dash absinthe

2 ounces soda water

½ teaspoon sugar

PROCEDURE

1. In a mixing glass ⅔ full of ice, stir cognac, rye whiskey, simple syrup, Cointreau, bitters, and absinthe. Add soda water.

2. Strain into a chilled highball glass.

3. Gently stir the sugar into the drink, which will cause the drink to foam up and form a head.

MORNING GLORY FIZZ

The Morning Glory Fizz is another hair-of-the-dog drink, but it's almost nothing like the similarly named Morning Glory Cocktail. One difference is that the Fizz calls for blended Scotch, unlike most of the other Scotch drinks detailed in this book. The Morning Glory Fizz first appeared in Harry Johnson's *New and Improved Bartender's Manual* in 1882, a time at which blended Scotch was only beginning to take off in Scotland. Very little of it was imported into the United States at the time, and so the drink probably initially used a single malt. Look for a higher proof spirit. Bottling Scotch at 80 proof is a fairly recent development, so try to find something around 90 to 100 proof, if you can.

INGREDIENTS

1 egg white (see pages 89–90 for tips on using raw eggs)

2 teaspoons superfine sugar

½ ounce lemon juice

¼ ounce lime juice

½ teaspoon absinthe

2 ounces rich blended Scotch (I like Great King Street)

1 ounce soda water

PROCEDURE

1. Add all ingredients except soda water to a shaker *without ice*.

2. Shake vigorously to combine egg white with other ingredients.

3. Add ice to shaker and shake vigorously again to chill and dilute the cocktail. Add soda water.

4. Strain into a highball glass without ice.

NEW YORK SOUR

Y'd think, from the name, that this drink hails from New York. But cocktail naming isn't any sort of science you can rely on. The New York Sour originated in Chicago in the 1880s, when a creative bartender decided to top a classic whiskey sour with a float of red wine. Surely the *name* comes from New York, right? Nope, that's from the Big Apple's other big rival, Boston. The cocktail first appeared in print under the name New York Sour in the *Boston Herald* newspaper in 1885.

The egg white here is optional; I prefer not to use it, actually, but some people find that it adds a silky texture. (Bartenders today are split on whether to include it; try it both ways and see what you prefer.) See pages 89–90 for tips on egg safety. If you omit the egg white, simply shake everything except the wine with ice, strain the drink into the prepared drinking glass, and float the wine.

For the red wine, choose something fruity and mildly spicy.

INGREDIENTS

2 ounces rye whiskey

1 ounce lemon juice

¾ ounce simple syrup

1 egg white

½ ounce red wine (look for Syrah, Shiraz, or Malbec)

PROCEDURE

1. Add rye whiskey, lemon juice, simple syrup, and egg white to a shaker *without ice*.

2. Shake vigorously to combine egg white with other ingredients.

3. Add ice to shaker and shake vigorously again to chill and dilute the cocktail.

4. Strain into a chilled coupe glass.

5. Using the back of a bar spoon, gently float the red wine atop the cocktail.

MANHATTAN, THREE WAYS

The history of the Manhattan, like with many cocktails, is a little murky. The drink first saw a print mention in 1882, even earlier than its gin cousin, the martini, during a period in which vermouth became an indispensable ingredient in the cocktail. No one has been able to pinpoint where it was created, though its origins on the island of Manhattan seem certain because every early account of the drink places it in various Manhattan bars or clubs.

I love a Manhattan, but only when it's made the right way. I insist on stirring it, so it stays clear and calm like a Zen garden. (Shaking it introduces a lot of fine bubbles that cloud its appearance and change its texture.)

I prefer a high proof rye or bourbon in a Manhattan so as to balance out the ample pour of vermouth that I suggest. Go for 100 proof Rittenhouse Rye or the bonded, 100 proof versions of Old Fitzgerald, Jim Beam, or Old Grand-Dad bourbons. Wild Turkey's 101 proof bourbon is also excellent in a manhattan.

I'm offering three variations here: the Classic Manhattan, the Dry Manhattan, and the Perfect Manhattan. What makes the Perfect perfect? Nothing, really. "Perfect" is simply an old bartender's term for a drink that calls for equal parts sweet vermouth and dry. Of the three Manhattans, I most prefer the Classic, though I also like the Perfect for a change of pace. Personally, I'm not a fan of the Dry, but I know people who love it and that is why I've included it here.

The classic garnish for a Manhattan is a cocktail cherry. Avoid the sugary-sweet maraschino cherries you can find at the grocery. Either use my recipe for homemade cherries, found on pages 208–209, or seek out the Luxardo brand.

CLASSIC MANHATTAN

INGREDIENTS

2 ounces high-proof rye whiskey or bourbon

1 ounce sweet vermouth

1 dash Angostura aromatic bitters

1 dash Angostura orange bitters

Cocktail cherry, for garnish

PROCEDURE

1. Pour whiskey, vermouth, and bitters into a chilled mixing glass.

2. Add enough cracked ice to fill mixing glass about ⅔ full.

3. Stir about 30 seconds, or until well-chilled.

4. Strain into a chilled cocktail glass.

5. Add garnish.

DRY MANHATTAN

INGREDIENTS

2 ounces high-proof rye whiskey or bourbon

1 ounce dry vermouth

1 dash Angostura aromatic bitters

1 dash Angostura orange bitters

Cocktail cherry, for garnish

PROCEDURE

1. Pour whiskey, vermouth, and bitters into a chilled mixing glass.

2. Add enough cracked ice to fill mixing glass about ⅔ full.

3. Stir about 30 seconds, or until well-chilled.

4. Strain into a chilled cocktail glass.

5. Add garnish.

PERFECT MANHATTAN

INGREDIENTS

2 ounces high-proof rye whiskey or bourbon

½ ounce sweet vermouth

½ ounce dry vermouth

1 dash Angostura aromatic bitters

1 dash Angostura orange bitters

Cocktail cherry, for garnish

PROCEDURE

1. Pour whiskey, sweet and dry vermouth, and bitters into a chilled mixing glass.

2. Add enough cracked ice to fill mixing glass about ⅔ full.

3. Stir about 30 seconds, or until well-chilled.

4. Strain into a chilled cocktail glass.

5. Add garnish.

OLD-FASHIONED

Rum makes a great old-fashioned, as do tequila, applejack, and brandy. Even gin is good in the drink. This, though, is a whiskey book, and pretty much any whiskey will work in an old-fashioned, though rye and bourbon are the classic stars.

In its later years, the old-fashioned took on fruit; cherries, slices of orange, and pineapple are common. And I'm sure some bartenders have thrown in starfruit, kiwifruit, bananas, kumquats, or whatever. None of these were present in the drink's origins. At most, early bartenders would muddle a strip of orange peel in the glass with the sugar and bitters. This is how I like to work it, too—I can't stand muddled cherries and orange pulp in my drink.

Debate rages as to whether bartenders should use granulated sugar or simple syrup in this drink. Sugar proponents argue that using sugar is the way the drink was first envisioned, and further, that muddling the sugar with the orange peel helps express oils from the peel into the drink, deepening its flavor. Simple syrup advocates say that syrup mixes more thoroughly into the cocktail, whereas sugar leaves a muddy residue in the glass. I present both versions here: you can make up your mind.

—•— THE ORIGINS OF —•—
THE WHISKEY COCKTAIL

Today we use the word *cocktail* to mean any mixed drink with alcohol in it. But initially, the word meant something more specific. The cocktail found its earliest known printed definition in 1806, in a Hudson, New York newspaper called *The Balance and Columbian Repository*. The paper's editor referred to a cocktail as a "bittered sling" and defined it as "a stimulating liquor, composed of spirits of any kind, sugar, water, and bitters."

This is precisely the recipe for the old-fashioned, at least in its early days. Originally called the whiskey cocktail, its recipe instructed the bartender to use the water and bitters to dissolve the sugar, add spirit of any kind, and stir, before adding ice and stirring again until cold. Eventually, cocktails became increasingly complicated, taking on any manner of ingredients, from absinthe to curaçao to vermouth. Soon enough, veteran topers longed for the old days of spirit, sugar, water, and bitters. And so they began asking for cocktails "in the old-fashioned style."

OLD-FASHIONED, WITH SUGAR

The classic. I sometimes like to mix one this way to remind myself of the drink's origins. The sugar sludge at the bottom is something that bothers some people and not others. I generally don't mind it, though I prefer the simple syrup version.

INGREDIENTS

1 sugar cube

Orange peel

1 dash Angostura bitters

1 teaspoon warm water

2 ounces rye whiskey or bourbon

PROCEDURE

1. In an old-fashioned glass, muddle sugar cube and orange peel to release the orange oils into the sugar.

2. Add bitters and warm water and muddle again to dissolve the sugar.

3. Add the whiskey and stir.

4. Add one large ice cube and stir again until chilled.

OLD-FASHIONED, WITH SIMPLE SYRUP

The updated classic. This version allows the sugar to incorporate fully into the drink.

INGREDIENTS

2 ounces rye whiskey or bourbon

1 teaspoon simple syrup

1 dash Angostura bitters

Orange peel, for garnish

PROCEDURE

1. In an old-fashioned glass, add whiskey, simple syrup, and bitters. Stir.

2. Add one large ice cube and stir again until chilled.

3. Twist the orange peel over the drink and drop it into the glass.

PRESBYTERIAN

The Presbyterian can be a ridiculously simple drink to make or it can be a little more complex, depending on how ambitious you feel in your home bar. I'll demonstrate both versions. Oh, why the name? No one knows. Such is the history of cocktails; it attempts to record things that happen while people are drinking. The drink dates probably to the 1890s, so there's not really anyone around from then to ask.

RIDICULOUSLY SIMPLE PRESBYTERIAN

INGREDIENTS

2 ounces blended Scotch whisky (I like The Famous Grouse Smoky Black, formerly known as The Black Grouse)

2 ounces spicy ginger ale (this drink needs a kick)

2 ounces club soda

PROCEDURE

1. Fill a collins glass with ice, and build the drink in the glass, pouring in all ingredients and stirring gently to combine.

LITTLE MORE COMPLEX PRESBYTERIAN

INGREDIENTS

2 ounces blended Scotch whisky

1 ounce Ginger Syrup (see recipe, page 204)

½ ounce lime juice

3 ounces club soda

PROCEDURE

1. In an ice-filled cocktail shaker, add Scotch, Ginger Syrup, and lime juice. Shake well until chilled and diluted. Add soda water.

2. Double strain (see page 87) into an ice-filled collins glass.

HORSE'S NECK

Originally a temperance drink of just ginger beer and a long spiral of lemon peel, this oddly named drink is a great cooler for a hot day. The drink is named for the lemon peel, which reportedly resembles a horse's neck. (I've never seen the similarities, personally.)

The drink dates back to before 1890, and it picked up American whiskey sometime around 1900. For the ginger beer, pick something spicy and sharp. A ginger ale will do as well, as long as the ginger offers enough bite to counteract the sweetness. To make the garnish, cut a long spiral from the lemon, using the entire peel, and place it in the glass before adding ice and the other ingredients.

INGREDIENTS

Peel of one lemon

2 ounces bourbon or rye whiskey

3 ounces ginger beer or ale

2 dashes Angostura bitters (optional, but tasty)

PROCEDURE

1. Place lemon peel into collins glass, and add ice.

2. Add other ingredients and stir gently to chill.

PRINCE EDWARD

Two cocktails in this book are named for Albert Edward, eldest son of Queen Victoria and later crowned King Edward VII. This first cocktail, the Prince Edward, has murky origins. Perhaps it owes its name to Albert Edward's playboy days prior to taking the crown. In any event, he was a renowned drinker.

The cocktail calls for blended Scotch (Johnnie Walker Red will do just fine), Lillet Blanc (an aperitif wine), and Drambuie. It's a simple drink, but a good one.

INGREDIENTS

1½ ounces blended Scotch whisky

½ ounce Lillet Blanc

¼ ounce Drambuie

Orange slice, for garnish

PROCEDURE

1. Fill a mixing glass ⅔ full of ice.

2. Add Scotch, Lillet, and Drambuie.

3. Stir about 30 seconds, or until well-chilled.

4. Strain into a chilled cocktail glass.

5. Add garnish.

ROB ROY

The drink most people think of when they think of Scotch cocktails, the Rob Roy is essentially a Scotch Manhattan. The drink arose in 1894 or 1895 and was named for a popular musical based on the life of the Scottish hero Robert Roy MacGregor. The place of origin for this drink is in dispute, but that's sadly common for cocktails.

If you're ever in Seattle, drop into the fine bar that takes its name from this drink and tell them I sent you.

INGREDIENTS

2 ounces blended Scotch whisky (I suggest The Famous Grouse)

1 ounce sweet vermouth

2 dashes orange bitters

Orange peel, for garnish

PROCEDURE

1. Fill a mixing glass ⅔ full of ice.

2. Add Scotch, vermouth, and bitters.

3. Stir about 30 seconds, or until well-chilled.

4. Strain into a chilled cocktail glass.

5. Add garnish.

ROCK AND RYE

A hundred years ago, you could step into most bars and order a Rock and Rye. This was a time when most rye and bourbon whiskeys were rough stuff and hard to enjoy on their own. Saloon keepers would mix up a batch of Rock and Rye to take the edge off the booze, and then sell it by the glass. Eventually, commercial bottlings were available on the market, though R and R's popularity began to fade after Prohibition, leaving only the bottommost of the bottom-shelf bottles still around. If you're a reader of a certain age, you might remember your grandmother offering it to you as a folk remedy for a sore throat. That's because, in the years before the Pure Food and Drug Act, Rock and Rye was marketed as medicine rather than as booze to get around the growing temperance movement of the 19th century.

Today, the craft cocktail community's commitment to exploring the history of hooch has led to a revival in R and R, with at least four commercial bottlings on the market as of 2015, and with more and more bartenders experimenting with house-made recipes.

A well-made Rock and Rye is like an old-fashioned in a bottle, with sugar, fruit, and a bittering flavor (in this case, horehound) complementing the spiciness of a good rye whiskey. Think of this as a premixed cocktail. A little work on a Sunday afternoon followed by some patience while the ingredients meld together will equal a good few nights of easy weeknight drinking.

I've taken a recipe that the Denver bar owner Sean Kenyon offered to *Imbibe* magazine and put my own spin on it. You can easily customize this recipe, swapping in other fruits and spices. The only essentials are rye whiskey, horehound, and rock candy. (Though, even there, you could sub in simple syrup or even sugar for the rock candy.)

INGREDIENTS

1 750-ml bottle rye whiskey (choose something high proof, like Rittenhouse 100 proof or Jim Beam 90 proof)

Peel of ½ orange

Peel of 1 whole lemon

2 slices orange

2 slices lemon

5 dried apricots

1 cinnamon stick

3 whole cloves

1 teaspoon dried horehound

1 (6-inch) string rock candy

TOOLS

Large glass jar

Fine strainer

Funnel

Empty 750-ml bottle

PROCEDURE

1. Combine all ingredients in large glass jar, except for cloves, horehound, and rock candy, and let infuse at room temperature for three days.

2. Add remaining ingredients and let infuse for 1 day.

3. Fine-strain and funnel into a clean glass bottle.

4. Keep refrigerated for up to two months.

PRINCE OF WALES

This drink is one of two cocktails named for Albert Edward, eldest son of Queen Victoria and later crowned King Edward VII. Cocktail historians believe that the Prince of Wales was invented by Albert Edward himself. During his mother's long reign, he had little to do aside from traveling, entertaining, and carrying on affairs with women of society. In other words, he had ample opportunity to enjoy fortified beverages. One of his own creation comes down to us as the Prince of Wales.

The drink calls for rye, bitters, maraschino liqueur, champagne, and a pineapple chunk. For this last ingredient, fresh pineapple is best, but you can use either canned or frozen. If using canned, rinse the syrup off first.

INGREDIENTS

1 cube of pineapple, about one inch per side

1 dash Angostura bitters

¼ ounce simple syrup

1½ ounces rye whiskey

¼ teaspoon maraschino liqueur

1 ounce chilled champagne

PROCEDURE

1. Muddle the pineapple, bitters, and simple syrup in a mixing glass.

2. Add rye and maraschino liqueur. Add ice. Close the shaker and shake until well-chilled and diluted.

3. Strain into a coupe glass and top with champagne.

WARD EIGHT

Though today Boston is one of the vibrant centers of the cocktail renaissance, for whatever reason, the city has played an undersized role in cocktail history. But Benton's history has given us two damn good things: the Hawthorne strainer (pages 77–78) and the Ward Eight cocktail. The story goes that the Ward Eight was invented to celebrate the 1898 election of a fellow from, well, Ward Eight. Regardless of its origins, think of this as a gussied-up Whiskey Sour (page 109), with the orange juice and grenadine adding a touch of sophistication to the drink.

INGREDIENTS

2 ounces rye whiskey

¾ ounce lemon juice

¾ ounce orange juice

1 teaspoon Grenadine (see recipe page 207)

PROCEDURE

1. Shake rye, both juices, and Grenadine in an ice-filled shaker.

2. Strain into a chilled cocktail glass.

SAZERAC

The Sazerac cocktail originated in New Orleans, during the latter half of the 19th century. No one's quite sure of the date, but the first printed reference to the drink appeared in 1898. Though today the drink is made with rye whiskey, the Sazerac was originally a cognac drink. With Louisiana having been originally a French colony, and New Orleans its port of entry, brandy and brandy-based cocktails were quite popular in New Orleans throughout the 19th century. The French influence also explains another ingredient in the drink, absinthe, which was also popular in New Orleans at that time.

Most of the pieces of the drink were in place long before its invention. The Sazerac, when you look at it, is not that far removed from an Improved Whiskey Cocktail (page 115). Drop the Improved's maraschino liqueur and add Peychaud's Bitters, and you have a Sazerac. The Peychaud in the bitters was from Antoine Amédée Peychaud, a Haitian apothecary who set up a druggist's shop in the French Quarter. At the time, bitters were seen as a type of medicine, sold for all sorts of ailments. But because they *were* so bitter, apothecaries would sell them mixed into alcoholic drinks. Peychaud devised his own brand of bitters and began using them in drinks. His brand still exists and still plays a crucial role in the Sazerac.

The drink itself takes its name from a brand of cognac that was imported into New Orleans at the time—Sazerac de Forge et Fils. By the beginning of the 20th century, however, rye whiskey was increasingly taking on the starring role. The American whiskey trade was thriving at this point, with shipments of bourbon and rye arriving regularly from Pennsylvania, Virginia, Tennessee, and Kentucky by way of the Ohio and Mississippi rivers. Whiskey cocktails became very popular in New Orleans by the beginning of the 20th century, and it seems that customers simply preferred the rye version of the drink to the cognac variety.

I tested several ryes for this recipe and decided I prefer Old Overholt in this drink. Bottled at 80 proof, it's mild enough to play well with the other flavors, but strong enough to assert the spicy flavors you associate with good rye whiskey. Higher proof ryes play well in other cocktails, such as the Manhattan (pages 120–122), but not in this drink. The bartender Naren Young, writing in *Imbibe* (UK) magazine, notes, "For this particular drink, though, which is served 'down' and therefore without ice, a lower proof whiskey . . . makes for a more balanced, sublime drink that does not burn away your taste buds."

The drink was formulated originally with absinthe, and though it was long banned in the United States, it's available again. There are many brands to choose from. However, the drink also works very well with Herbsaint, an absinthe substitute invented in 1934. Look for the original formulation, with is bottled at 100 proof. You might have to mail order it, but don't feel bad; it's great in the Cocktail *à la Louisiane,* too (page 188).

Mixing a Sazerac is as much about ritual as it is about technique, which I detail below. Whenever I feel nostalgic for the French Quarter, I put on the Tom Waits song, "I Wish I Was in New Orleans" and mix a Sazerac.

INGREDIENTS

Few drops absinthe or absinthe substitute

2½ ounces rye whiskey

1 teaspoon simple syrup

3 dashes Peychaud's Bitters

1 dash Angostura bitters

Lemon peel, for garnish

PROCEDURE

1. Into a prechilled old-fashioned glass, pour a few drops of absinthe. Roll it around inside the glass to coat the sides and bottom. Pour out the excess, but leave a tiny bit on the bottom of the glass. Set aside.

2. In a second old-fashioned glass, add ice cubes, whiskey, simple syrup, and both bitters. Stir until well-chilled.

3. Strain into the absinthe-coated glass.

4. Squeeze the lemon peel over the surface of the glass, rub the rim with the peel, and discard the peel.

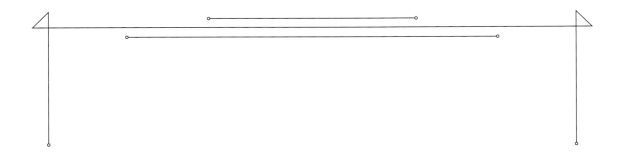

1900–1920

PRE-PROHIBITION
WHISKEY COCKTAILS

BROOKLYN

The poor Brooklyn cocktail. It's taken a lot of abuse over the years. But the worst thing that ever happened to it was the introduction of dry vermouth. Don't do it. Just don't. The original 1908 formulation, by a barman named Jack Grohusko, called for sweet vermouth, which is much better with rye whiskey than dry vermouth.

Grohusko also calls for Amer Picon, which is unavailable in the United States and is, at any rate, a poor shadow of its former self, even if you *can* find it. The best current substitute is Amaro CioCiaro (*amaro* is Italian for "bitter"), gussied up with a dash of orange bitters.

INGREDIENTS

1½ ounces rye whiskey (go with something high proof)

1½ ounces sweet vermouth

½ teaspoon Amaro CioCiaro

½ teaspoon maraschino liqueur

1 dash Regan's Orange Bitters

Lemon peel, for garnish

PROCEDURE

1. Pour whiskey, vermouth, amaro, maraschino liqueur, and orange bitters into a chilled mixing glass.

2. Add enough cracked ice to fill mixing glass about ⅔ full.

3. Stir about 30 seconds, or until well-chilled.

4. Strain into a chilled cocktail glass.

5. Twist lemon peel over cocktail, rub the peel on the rim, and drop into the glass.

BOBBY BURNS

One of the finest chroniclers of the early American cocktail was a man named Albert Stevens Crockett, a newspaperman born in the 1870s. As is common among journalists, he liked to tip his elbow. He ultimately contributed two volumes to cocktail literature: *Old Waldorf Bar Days* and *The Old Waldorf-Astoria Bar Book*. (The Waldorf and the Astoria were once separate hotels, and neighbors on the site now occupied by the Empire State Building.) Both books came out post-Prohibition, but both detail the drinks served at the hotels prior to the Volstead Act.

Nearly every publication that features a recipe for the Bobby Burns claims that it is named for the Scottish poet Robert Burns. Crockett suggests another theory, though he makes it clear he doesn't know the answer either. He says there was a cigar on the market in the early 20th century called Bobby Burns, and one of its salesmen used to drop a lot of money at the Waldorf bar. By this account, the drink is named to honor this salesman's spending habits.

Regardless of the origin of its name, the Bobby Burns cocktail features—no surprise—Scotch. For the liqueur, both Bénédictine and Drambuie work well, so just pick one and go with it.

INGREDIENTS

2 ounces blended whiskey (I like The Famous Grouse)

1 ounce sweet vermouth

1 dash Peychaud's Bitters

2 dashes Bénédictine or Drambuie

Lemon peel, for garnish

PROCEDURE

1. Pour whiskey, vermouth, bitters, and Bénédictine into a chilled mixing glass.

2. Add enough cracked ice to fill mixing glass about ⅔ full.

3. Stir about 30 seconds, or until well-chilled.

4. Strain into a chilled cocktail glass.

5. Twist lemon peel over cocktail, rub the peel on the rim, and drop into the glass.

FANCIULLI

The Fanciulli is essentially a Manhattan variation that calls for Fernet-Branca. Fernet is a type of amaro (bitter spirit), and Branca is the brand name. Fernets are intensely herbal, and were originally formulated as a digestive aid. Fernets usually include myrrh, rhubarb, chamomile, aloe, and saffron, among other ingredients. Branca is specifically also minty.

I sometimes enjoy a fernet as an after-dinner drink to combat the indigestion of a heavy meal (I especially enjoy a few sips on Thanksgiving night). But I prefer it as a cocktail ingredient, and I find that a strong bourbon whiskey tames it very well. Another good foil for fernet? A spicy sweet vermouth: try Vya, Punt e Mes or Carpano Antica.

The Fanciulli, like the Bobby Burns (page 141), is another contribution from the Waldorf bar. And the bar's champion, the venerable A. S. Crockett, dates its creation to no later than 1910.

INGREDIENTS

2 ounces bourbon whiskey (I suggest Bulleit)

¾ ounce sweet vermouth

¼ ounce Fernet-Branca

PROCEDURE

1. Fill a mixing glass ⅔ full of ice.

2. Add bourbon, vermouth, and Fernet-Branca, and stir 15 seconds, or until chilled and diluted.

3. Strain into a chilled cocktail glass.

MODERN COCKTAIL #1

It once was common in cocktail books to find drinks that share a name. The best-known example of this might be the Corpse Reviver #1 and the Corpse Reviver #2—two very different drinks with a common moniker.

The Modern Cocktail also fits this bill. A version from Hugo Ensslin's 1917 book *Recipes for Mixed Drinks* calls for Scotch and Jamaican rum. That one comes to us as the Modern #1, presented below. The #2, on the pages following, uses Scotch and sloe gin. Try them both and see which you prefer.

INGREDIENTS

2 ounces blended Scotch (try The Famous Grouse)

¼ ounce Jamaican rum (try Appleton Estate)

¼ ounce lemon juice

1 dash absinthe

1 dash orange bitters

PROCEDURE

1. Shake all ingredients in an ice-filled shaker.

2. Strain into a chilled cocktail glass.

MODERN COCKTAIL #2

The Hoffman House hotel, formerly at Broadway and 25th Street in Manhattan, had what was once the finest bar in New York City. Many famous bartenders worked there, including Harry Craddock, who fled the country during Prohibition to head up the American Bar at the Savoy Hotel in London. Among the classic cocktails invented at the Hoffman were the Hoffman House, Police Gazette, and Elks' Fizz. In 1912, the head bartender, Charles Mahoney, wrote a book about the hotel's famed bar, *Hoffman House Bartender's Guide: How to Open a Saloon and Make It Pay*. The Modern #2 appears therein.

INGREDIENTS

1 ounce blended Scotch (Johnnie Walker Black's smokiness is great here)

1 ounce sloe gin (Plymouth makes a great version)

1½ teaspoons lemon juice

1 teaspoon superfine sugar

1 dash absinthe

1 dash orange bitters

PROCEDURE

1. Shake all ingredients in an ice-filled shaker.

2. Strain into a chilled cocktail glass.

TIPPERARY

The Bijou is a gin cocktail from the 1800s, calling for gin, green Chartreuse, and sweet vermouth. It's one of my favorite gin drinks, but this obviously isn't a gin book. Thankfully, we have the Tipperary, a variation that arose just before Prohibition. As the name might imply, it uses Irish whiskey instead of English gin.

There are two ways to make this drink, and which you choose depends on your own taste. You can keep the Chartreuse in the cocktail, or you can rinse the serving glass with it and discard the rest. Keeping it in results in a slightly sweeter and more herbally complex drink. Discarding it gives a drier, more subtle cocktail. Wouldn't hurt to try it both ways.

For the whiskey, I suggest a rich, pot-stilled whiskey like Redbreast or Jameson Black Barrel.

INGREDIENTS

½ ounce green Chartreuse

2 ounces Irish whiskey

1 ounce sweet vermouth

PROCEDURE

1. Into a chilled cocktail glass, pour the green Chartreuse. Swirl it around to coat the sides of the glass. Either discard it or keep it, depending on how sweet you want the cocktail.

2. Fill a mixing glass ⅔ full of ice.

3. Add whiskey and vermouth.

4. Stir about 30 seconds, or until well-chilled.

5. Pour into glass.

SEELBACH

The Seelbach Hotel in Louisville, Kentucky opened in 1905. Its location near the heart of the bourbon industry attracted gamblers and gangsters, and then—during Prohibition—bootleggers. Writers, too: F. Scott Fitzgerald frequented the hotel while stationed at nearby Camp Taylor, and the ballroom inspired a wedding scene in *The Great Gatsby*.

The cocktail named for the hotel was born here, too, although it was served for the last time right before Prohibition. In 1995, the hotel's restaurant director rediscovered the recipe and began serving the drink in the hotel bar. He wanted to keep the recipe secret, but the cocktail writers Gary and Mardee Regan persuaded him to offer up the recipe, and then published it in their *New Classic Cocktails*.

The amount of bitters in the recipe may look like a typo. I assure you, it's not. The bitters add a nice herbal complexity to the drink. For the wine, I like Gruet Brut from New Mexico; it's suitably champagne-like, but much less expensive.

INGREDIENTS

1 ounce bourbon (the hotel uses Old Forester)

½ ounce Cointreau

4 dashes Angostura bitters

3 dashes Peychaud's Bitters

5 ounces domestic sparkling wine

Long lemon peel, for garnish

PROCEDURE

1. Stir bourbon, Cointreau, and both bitters in a mixing glass filled with ice.

2. Strain into a champagne flute. Top with sparkling wine.

3. Squeeze the lemon peel over the surface of the glass, rub the rim with the peel, and drop the peel into the glass.

MAMIE TAYLOR

I have a strange fondness for cocktails named after people. Admittedly, it's a risky move because a cocktail named for a person can feel dated and stodgy, especially if the person is largely forgotten, like Ms. Taylor is today. Mayme Taylor (note the spelling variation) was a singer in musical theater. Some have even called her an opera singer, though it's unclear whether that part's true. Writing in the *Wall Street Journal,* the cocktail historian Eric Felten tells us that in the early 1900s both the drink and its inspiration were once almost universally famous in the United States. Both then fell on hard times and are now nearly forgotten.

The drink of the time was almost certainly made with blended Scotch. Blends today are generally milder tasting than they were a century ago. Indeed, many modern blends are too mild to stand up to ginger beer, especially a spicy one. I like the Great King Street blends from Compass Box, and they should be relatively easy to find. Otherwise, The Famous Grouse Smoky Black blend would work well.

INGREDIENTS

2 ounces Scotch

¾ ounce lime juice

Spicy ginger ale or ginger beer

Lime wedge, for garnish

PROCEDURE

1. Add Scotch, lime juice, and ginger ale to a highball glass full of ice.

2. Stir briefly and garnish with a lime wedge.

POLICE GAZETTE COCKTAIL

The *National Police Gazette* was an American magazine, founded in 1845, that chronicled the activities of criminals from across the country. Later in its existence, it reported the results of boxing matches and other sporting events, and also covered the social lives of actresses and chorus girls. In fact, in covering sports and gossip, the *Gazette* was an innovator, pioneering the concept of the sports page and the gossip column. The *Gazette* covered pugilists and prostitutes, theater and thuggery—anything that 19th-century Americans saw as sinful and that the *Gazette* saw as business.

Included in this roundup of vice was the tavern and the saloon industry, and the *Gazette* dutifully chronicled the emergence of an emergent American craft, the cocktail. The *Gazette* frequently held cocktail contests in its pages, inviting saloon owners and bartenders to submit drink recipes for consideration. The Police Gazette Cocktail was one of the drinks sent in, though no one knows now who sent it in, or when.

The cocktail first appears in the 1901 *New Police Gazette Bartenders Guide.* Note the use of *dashes* for ingredients that don't normally come in dasher bottles. For 3 dashes, use a scant ¼ teaspoon of the ingredient (which means don't quite fill up the spoon), and for 2 dashes, use even a scantier ¼ teaspoon.

INGREDIENTS

2½ ounces rye whiskey

2 dashes French vermouth

3 dashes simple syrup

2 dashes Angostura bitters

2 dashes Cointreau

2 dashes maraschino liqueur

PROCEDURE

1. Pour ingredients into a chilled mixing glass.

2. Add enough cracked ice to fill mixing glass about ⅔ full.

3. Stir about 30 seconds, or until well-chilled.

4. Strain into a chilled cocktail glass.

CABLEGRAM

The Cablegram cocktail was created during Prohibition, and the first writing of it appears in *The Savoy Cocktail Book* by Harry Craddock. Old Harry called for taking whiskey, lemon juice, and sugar and making a whiskey sour, and then adding ginger ale to create a "long" drink—that is, one that's served in a tall glass with a mixer to make it a longer-sipping drink. That version's fine—spicy and refreshing, especially on a hot day.

Even better, I think, is a modern iteration created by Eric Alperin at The Varnish bar in Los Angeles. This version uses homemade ginger syrup to create a fresher, sharper ginger flavor, and lime juice in place of lemon, simply because lime juice tastes better with ginger than does lemon.

INGREDIENTS

2 ounces rye whiskey

¾ ounce Ginger Syrup (see recipe, page 204)

½ ounce lime juice

1 ounce soda water

Candied ginger, for garnish

PROCEDURE

1. Add whiskey, Ginger Syrup, and lime juice to an ice-filled cocktail shaker. Shake until well-mixed. Add soda water.

2. Fine-strain into an ice-filled collins glass.

3. Add garnish.

CAMERON'S KICK

This is an unusual drink in that it combines Scotch and Irish whiskeys. Orgeat is an almond syrup deepened with a hint of orange water. Torani's version is widely available, but if you can find the B. G. Reynolds's bottling, use that.

INGREDIENTS

1 ounce blended Scotch (I like The Famous Grouse)

1 ounce Irish whiskey (I like Black Bush)

½ ounce lemon juice

½ ounce orgeat syrup

PROCEDURE

1. Shake all ingredients in an ice-filled shaker.

2. Strain into a chilled cocktail glass.

CREOLE COCKTAIL

Little is known about the origins of the Creole cocktail, except that it's a variation on the Manhattan (pages 120–122). Bénédictine adds herbal complexity, and the amaro provides a bitter punch. The original recipe called for Amer Picon, which is unavailable in the United States. The best easily obtained substitute is Amaro CioCiaro.

INGREDIENTS

1 ounce rye whiskey

1 ounce sweet vermouth

2 dashes Bénédictine

2 dashes Amaro CioCiaro

1 dash orange bitters

Lemon peel, for garnish

PROCEDURE

1. In a mixing glass filled ⅔ with ice, stir rye, vermouth, Bénédictine, amaro, and orange bitters.

2. Strain into a chilled cocktail glass.

3. Squeeze the lemon peel over the surface of the glass, rub the rim with the peel, and drop the peel into the glass.

OLD PAL

On one level, this looks like a variation on the Boulevardier (page 156), which calls for bourbon or rye, Campari, and sweet vermouth. Old Pal is certainly a close cousin, with its rye, Campari, and dry vermouth. But the Old Pal, thanks to the dry vermouth, is less sweet than the Boulevardier. Also, though I love the Boulevardier, the Old Pal's dry vermouth does a somewhat better job of marrying the whiskey and Campari.

INGREDIENTS

1½ ounces rye whiskey

¾ ounce dry vermouth

¾ ounce Campari

Lemon peel, for garnish

PROCEDURE

1. Fill a mixing glass ⅔ full of ice.

2. Add whiskey, vermouth, and Campari.

3. Stir about 30 seconds, or until well-chilled.

4. Strain into a chilled cocktail glass.

5. Squeeze the lemon peel over the surface of the glass, rub the rim with the peel, and drop the peel into the glass.

PADDY

The Irish answer to the Manhattan, the Paddy mixes Irish whiskey with sweet vermouth and Angostura bitters. The origin is unknown, but it appears in *The Savoy Cocktail Book* from 1930, so it's been around a while.

INGREDIENTS

2 ounces Irish whiskey (I suggest Black Bush)

¾ ounce sweet vermouth

2 dashes Angostura bitters

Cherry, for garnish

PROCEDURE

1. Fill a mixing glass ⅔ full of ice.

2. Add whiskey, vermouth, and bitters.

3. Stir about 30 seconds, or until well-chilled.

4. Strain into a chilled cocktail glass.

5. Add garnish.

REMEMBER THE MAINE

One of the most iconoclastic travel and food writers of the 20th century was Charles Henry Baker Jr. Born in 1895, he was a writer, magazine editor, and world traveler, who contributed to *Esquire*, *Town & Country*, and *Gourmet* magazines. But he's known today for his books, each of which is one part memoir, one part travelogue, and one part recipe book.

Baker took three world tours, recording his experiences with food and drink wherever he went. In 1939, he published his first book, a two-volume set called *The Gentleman's Companion*. The first volume is a cookbook. But it's the second that interests us most, a volume subtitled *Being an Exotic Drinking Book or, Around the World with Jigger, Beaker and Flask*. In this book, Baker describes cocktails from around the world, discusses a bit about them, and provides recipes. Many of his recipes are garbage, the cocktails being nearly undrinkable, though his prose style is uniquely charming. The Maine, however, is a forever keeper. It's a drink you'll never want to stop enjoying.

Here's how he describes it:

> REMEMBER the MAINE, a Hazy Memory of a Night in Havana during the Unpleasantnesses of 1933, when Each Swallow Was Punctuated with Bombs Going off on the Prado, or the Sound of 3" Shells Being Fired at the Hotel NACIONAL, then Haven for Certain Anti-Revolutionary Officers.

INGREDIENTS

2 ounces rye whiskey

¾ ounce sweet vermouth

2 teaspoons Cherry Heering liqueur

½ teaspoon absinthe

Cherry, for garnish

PROCEDURE

1. Add all ingredients but garnish to a mixing glass, filled with cracked ice. Stir well for about 30 seconds.

2. Strain into a chilled cocktail glass. Add garnish.

TWELVE MILE LIMIT

Here is a Prohibition-era cocktail named, cheekily, for a Prohibition-era law. When Prohibition went into effect in 1920, the Coast Guard began enforcing a blockade to prevent ships from bringing alcoholic beverages to shore. At first, the blockade was set three miles out from shore, but this distance was short enough that small watercraft (even human-powered rowboats) could approach large ships at night and clandestinely load up with illicit hooch. In 1924, Congress passed a law extending the distance to twelve miles, making such excursions beyond the reach of only the most-resourceful bootleggers.

As you'll soon learn, the Prohibition inspired the name of one cocktail, the Scofflaw. At least two more took their names from the law: the Three Mile Limit and the Twelve Mile Limit. The first drink is not of interest to us right now; it has no whiskey. The latter cocktail, though, is just the sort of boozy delight you'd hoist to thumb your nose at the law. The base is rum, but there's just enough rye in there to remind you how good rye is.

The drink, by the way, is credited to a journalist named Tommy Millard. I've bellied the bar with many a journalist, and this is just the sort of thing they love.

INGREDIENTS

1 ounce white rum (use El Dorado 3 Year Old, if you can find it)

½ ounce rye whiskey

½ ounce cognac (Hennessy will do the trick)

½ ounce Grenadine (see recipe, page 207)

½ ounce lemon juice

Lemon peel, for garnish

PROCEDURE

1. Shake liquors, Grenadine, and lemon juice in an ice-filled shaker.

2. Strain into a chilled cocktail glass.

3. Squeeze the lemon peel over the surface of the glass, rub the rim with the peel, and drop the peel into the glass.

WHISKEY

SCOFFLAW

While the United States was on boozy lockdown during Prohibition, tipplers across the Atlantic were still having drinky fun—and poking fun at their dry American cousins. The Scofflaw cocktail was one such taunt. It arose in 1924 at Harry's New York Bar in Paris.

INGREDIENTS

1½ ounces rye whiskey

1 ounce dry vermouth

¾ ounce lemon juice

¾ ounce Grenadine (see recipe, page 207)

Lemon peel, for garnish

PROCEDURE

1. To an ice-filled cocktail shaker, add rye whiskey, vermouth, lemon juice, and Grenadine.

2. Shake well for at least 30 seconds to blend and dilute the cocktail.

3. Strain into an ice-filled rocks glass.

4. Squeeze the lemon peel over the surface of the glass, rub the rim with the peel, and drop the peel into the glass.

TORONTO

In the Toronto drink, we have an old-fashioned variation that calls for Fernet-Branca. As described in the Fanciulli recipe, Fernet-Branca is bitter and intensely herbal. It arose in Italy in the mid-1800s. And when Italians emigrated to Canada in the 1920s, many of them settled in Toronto, where they enjoyed a cocktail made with Canadian whisky and Italian amaro.

You'll see a lot of recipes for this drink that call for American rye whiskey, primarily because it does such a great job of taming Fernet-Branca's big personality. But the name of the drink doesn't suggest America *or* its whiskeys, does it?

No, the drink, as it was first devised, called for Canadian whisky. And I think given its name, we owe it to the Toronto to provide it its native tipple. But pick something with some flavor! Many Canadian brands are too tame for Branca. I mix mine using a true Canadian rye, the Dark Batch release from Alberta. If you can find Forty Creek, that would work, too.

INGREDIENTS

2 ounces rye whiskey (I suggest Dark Batch)

¼ ounce Fernet-Branca

¼ ounce simple syrup

2 dashes Angostura bitters

Orange peel, for garnish

PROCEDURE

1. Fill a mixing glass ⅔ full of ice.

2. Add rye, Fernet-Branca, simple syrup, and bitters, and stir 15 seconds, or until chilled and diluted.

3. Strain into a chilled cocktail glass, and add garnish.

LION'S TAIL

Here's a drink that uses an ingredient that entirely disappeared, for a time, from the American cocktail landscape. Allspice dram, also known as pimento dram, is a Jamaican ingredient made by steeping allspice berries in rum. (In Jamaica, allspice is known as *pimento*, even though it has nothing to do with the little red peppers stuffed into olives that we associate with the word *pimento*.)

A company called Haus Alpenz imports St. Elizabeth Allspice Dram, and it should be fairly easy to track down. Though allspice dram is most typically used in rum-based tiki drinks, its pungent flavors of nutmeg and clove and cinnamon marry well with bourbon.

INGREDIENTS

2 ounces bourbon

¾ ounce allspice dram

½ ounce lime juice

½ tablespoon simple syrup

2 dashes Angostura bitters

PROCEDURE

1. Add all ingredients to an ice-filled shaker.

2. Shake for 20 seconds and strain into a chilled cocktail glass.

1933–1999

POST-PROHIBITION
WHISKEY COCKTAILS

ALGONQUIN

Look around the Internet for this cocktail, and you'll discover that nearly everyone who mentions it repeats the same old story: It's named for the Algonquin Hotel (where, from 1919 to 1929, Dorothy Parker and other writers of the time had a famous and long-term lunch date). Only problem is, no one knows whether that's actually true. The recipe first appears in the 1930s, and no one writing at the time bothered to attempt to document its origin.

Other things in this world named *Algonquin* include a tribe of Native Americans, a hotel in Canada, a radio observatory also in Canada, a club in Boston, a French ship, two Canadian ships, and three American ships, not to mention several towns in the United States and Canada. The cocktail could have been named for any one of those things. The only thing I'm reasonably certain *didn't* inspire the drink's name is a high school in Massachusetts, not least because the school wasn't established until 1959. I do find it amusing to think, though, that some subversive wag might have named a high school after a cocktail.

Did Parker and her cohorts drink this cocktail? Maybe? Probably not? No one really knows, and it doesn't really matter. If you like it, drink it and make up whatever story you want.

INGREDIENTS

1½ ounces rye whiskey

¾ ounce French vermouth

¾ ounce unsweetened pineapple juice

Orange peel, for garnish

PROCEDURE

1. Pour whiskey, vermouth, and pineapple juice into a chilled mixing glass.

2. Add enough cracked ice to fill mixing glass about ⅔ full.

3. Stir about 30 seconds, or until well-chilled.

4. Strain into a chilled cocktail glass.

5. Twist orange peel over cocktail, rub the peel on the rim, and drop into the glass.

DIAMONDBACK

An obscure drink that deserves a comeback. This cocktail is my adaptation of a drink that arose in Baltimore some time prior to 1951, when it appeared in Ted Saucier's book *Bottoms Up,* calling for rye whiskey, applejack, and yellow Chartreuse. Fifty-some years later, a Seattle bartender, Murray Stenson, revived the drink, using green Chartreuse in place of the yellow. This was wise: The green has more herbal complexity and brings more flavor to the drink.

Be careful with your ingredients. I like the 100 proof bottling of Laird's Applejack here; I think the blended 80 proof lacks the flavor you need with two other strong ingredients. But the Chartreuse clocks in at 110 proof. You *could* choose a 100 proof rye, such as Rittenhouse here, and I've done that before. But that's a boozy damn drink, probably too boozy. Go with a rye that's a little lighter, such as Sazerac.

INGREDIENTS

1½ ounces rye whiskey (I prefer Sazerac)

1 ounce 100-proof applejack

½ ounce green Chartreuse

Cocktail cherry, for garnish

PROCEDURE

1. Fill a mixing glass ⅔ full of ice.

2. Add all ingredients except the garnish.

3. Stir about 30 seconds, until diluted and well-chilled.

4. Strain into an ice-filled old-fashioned glass. Add garnish.

MOTHER-IN-LAW

Here's an odd duck. The Mother-in-Law cocktail is a bottled cocktail, devised in New Orleans some time prior to World War I. The inventor wasn't a bartender but Jeannette Lyons, a socialite and the wife of a prominent New Orleans druggist. Mrs. Lyons mixed these by the quart, and later passed the recipe down to her daughter-in-law, who in turn passed it down to her grandson. The ingredients are generally straightforward, though the original recipe called for Amer Picon, which is unavailable in the United States. You can substitute in either Torani Amer or Amaro CioCiara.

INGREDIENTS

2½ teaspoons Peychaud's Bitters

2½ teaspoons Angostura bitters

2½ teaspoons Torani Amer

1½ ounces maraschino liqueur (Luxardo or Maraska)

1½ ounces Cointreau or high-quality orange curaçao

1½ ounces simple syrup

One 750-ml bottle Buffalo Trace bourbon

Cherry, for garnish

PROCEDURE

1. Combine ingredients, except the cherry, thoroughly and pour into a clean one-quart bottle.

2. To serve, pour three ounces into a mixing glass with cracked ice.

3. Stir for no less than 30 seconds, then strain into a cocktail glass.

4. Garnish with a stemless cherry.

LEATHERNECK

I'm including this cocktail in part because it amuses me to do so. A "leatherneck" is, in slang, a Marine—a member of either the United States Marine Corps or the British Royal Marines. The nickname refers to the high leather collar that shielded the necks of Marines in the Revolutionary War. So you'd expect this to be a tough-guy drink, probably made from Jack Daniel's and liquid testosterone. Ha! The drink, strangely, calls for one of the mildest whiskeys around: blended North American.

Oh, and? The drink is blue. It could, I suppose, refer to a Marine's dress blues, but it's not the proper shade of blue for that. Also, blue drinks are not traditionally considered macho.

To my own personal surprise, the drink is tasty, which is the other reason why it's here. It's a colorful whiskey sour; those are hard to screw up.

For another variation of this concept, try Kazuo Ueda's **King's Valley**: 2 ounces blended Scotch, ½ ounce Cointreau, ½ ounce lime juice, and ¼ ounce blue curaçao. Prepare it the same way as the Leatherneck.

INGREDIENTS

2 ounces blended whiskey (Crown Royal or Canadian Club will work)

¾ ounce blue curaçao

¼ ounce lime juice

PROCEDURE

1. To an ice-filled cocktail shaker, add blended whiskey, curaçao, and lime juice.

2. Shake well for at least 30 seconds to blend and dilute the cocktail.

3. Strain into a chilled cocktail glass.

GODFATHER

This 1970s-era drink, named for the popular film *The Godfather,* is a simple mix of whiskey and amaretto. The original specification was for equal parts, but I find that too sweet. I've included my favorite proportion, but feel free to tinker around until you find yours.

INGREDIENTS

2 ounces blended Scotch or bourbon

¼ ounce amaretto

PROCEDURE

1. Fill a mixing glass ⅔ full of ice. Add ingredients and stir until chilled.

2. Strain into ice-filled rocks glass.

IRISH COFFEE

Transatlantic flight in the early 1940s was much different than we know it today. The only planes that could make the jump were so-called flying boats that could fly only between marine-based airports. Flying west from Europe first meant getting to Southampton on the southern England coast. From there, you'd fly to Foynes in the west of Ireland, where you'd stop over for refueling. Then a hop across the Atlantic would take you to Botwood, Newfoundland, where you'd refuel again, before flying on to New Brunswick and then into New York.

One such flight left Foynes on a winter's night in 1943. The weather was rough and the captain decided to return to Foynes to await better conditions. He sent a Morse code message ahead to the tower to alert them to await his passengers. The chef of the Foynes airport restaurant, a man named Joe Sheridan, whipped up hot food and drinks for the returning passengers. And to provide extra fortification against the elements, he spiked their coffees with Irish whiskey and topped them with the rich cream, lightly whipped, that Irish dairy cows were known for.

Irish coffee only needs four ingredients: brown sugar, Irish whiskey, good coffee, and cream. Irish coffee doesn't need vanilla, Bailey's, espresso, butterscotch, caramel, pumpkin spice, cocoa, or any of the other nonsense that people sometimes insist on.

For the whiskey, I like Black Bush from Bushmills for a good Irish coffee. For an even better Irish coffee, I love Redbreast. Brown sugar is necessary because it gives the coffee enough viscosity to float cream atop. Any basic brown will do, but I prefer using turbinado (or sugar in the raw). Don't fret the coffee, just use something you really like. Make sure your cream is fresh and rich, unsweetened, and very lightly whipped.

INGREDIENTS

1½ ounces Irish whiskey

1 tablespoon brown sugar

3 ounces hot black coffee

1 ounce heavy cream, lightly whipped

PROCEDURE

1. Fill an Irish coffee glass with boiling water. Let it sit for 30 seconds to warm the glass and dump the water.

2. Add whiskey, brown sugar, and coffee to the glass and stir until sugar melts.

3. Pour whipped cream over the back of a spoon onto the top of the coffee, so that it floats atop.

4. *Do not stir the cream into the coffee.* As you sip, allow the coffee to come up through the cream; they'll slowly mingle as you drink.

MONTE CARLO

The Monte Carlo is simply another variation on a Manhattan. Its origins are unknown. To make it, you swap out the Manhattan's vermouth and use Bénédictine instead. Bénédictine is an herbal liqueur, made by monks using a secret formula that includes herbs, spices, and other aromatic ingredients. Bénédictine is quite sweet, and so a little goes a long way. I like using a high proof rye for this, such as Rittenhouse, at 100 proof.

INGREDIENTS

2 ounces rye whiskey

½ ounce Bénédictine

1 dash Angostura bitters

PROCEDURE

1. Fill a mixing glass ⅔ full of ice.

2. Add all ingredients.

3. Stir about 30 seconds, or until well-chilled.

4. Strain into a chilled cocktail glass.

PREAKNESS

You think the Derby is the only horserace with a drink all its own? Well, maybe it is. After all, the official drink of the Preakness Stakes is now the Black-Eyed Susan, and the less said about that drink, the better. The Preakness was once the official drink of the Preakness, debuting in 1936, and it's a shame it's not still—it's by far the better drink. It may be yet another riff on the Manhattan, but it's an especially good one, with herbal Bénédictine contributing flavors you don't get in your typical Manhattan.

INGREDIENTS

1½ ounces rye whiskey

¾ ounce sweet vermouth

¼ ounce Bénédictine

1 dash Angostura bitters

Lemon peel, for garnish

PROCEDURE

1. Fill a mixing glass ⅔ full of ice.

2. Add whiskey, vermouth, Bénédictine, and bitters.

3. Stir about 30 seconds, or until well-chilled.

4. Strain into a chilled cocktail glass.

5. Squeeze the lemon peel over the surface of the glass, rub the rim with the peel, and drop the peel into the glass.

RUSTY NAIL

A simple, two-ingredient drink, the Rusty Nail combines Scotch and Drambuie, a liqueur made of Scotch, honey, and herbs. The drink traditionally calls for equal parts of the two ingredients, but I find that too sweet. Better to start with a 4:1 ratio and add more Drambuie if you need it.

INGREDIENTS

2 ounces blended Scotch (I suggest Johnny Walker Black)

½ ounce Drambuie

PROCEDURE

1. Add both ingredients to a rocks glass filled with ice. Stir well to chill.

VIEUX CARRÉ

Invented in 1938 by Walter Bergeron at the Hotel Monteleone in New Orleans, the Vieux Carré is named for the city's French Quarter. (*Vieux carré* is French for "old square," another name for the Quarter.) The drink is a riff on the Old-Fashioned (pages 124–125), and it pays homage to the city's French and American heritage by featuring cognac, rye, Bénédictine (an herbal French liqueur), and Peychaud's Bitters, the New Orleans classic found also in the Sazerac (pages 136–137).

INGREDIENTS

1 ounce rye whiskey (Sazerac rye is good in this)

1 ounce cognac (Hennessy will work just fine)

1 ounce sweet vermouth

1 teaspoon Bénédictine herbal liqueur

2 dashes Peychaud's Bitters

2 dashes Angostura bitters

PROCEDURE

1. Add all ingredients to an ice-filled rocks glass. Stir.

COCKTAIL À LA LOUISIANE

The signature cocktail of the Restaurant de la Louisiane (which opened in New Orleans in 1881 and is now a catering hall), this is a relative of the Vieux Carré, another Big Easy classic. This is a short drink, just over two ounces, so have a couple. You'll thank me.

The drink first appeared in print in Stanley Clisby Arthur's *Famous New Orleans Drinks* from 1937. This book appeared during a time when true absinthe was banned in the United States, and just after the absinthe substitute Herbsaint hit the market. Herbsaint was invented in New Orleans and has always been quite popular there. I can't prove it, but I'd bet money that old Stan had Herbsaint in mind when he published this recipe. As I mentioned when discussing the Sazerac (pages 136–137), look for the original formulation, with is bottled at 100 proof.

It's hard to tell when the drink was invented, though when *Famous New Orleans Drinks* was published, it was on the restaurant's menu, so I'm going to peg it as a post-Prohibition creation.

INGREDIENTS

¾ **ounce rye whiskey**

¾ **ounce Italian vermouth**

¾ **ounce Bénédictine**

3 dashes Herbsaint, pastis, or other absinthe substitute

3 dashes Peychaud's Bitters

Cocktail cherry, for garnish

PROCEDURE

1. Fill a mixing glass ⅔ full of ice.

2. Add whiskey, vermouth, Bénédictine, Herbsaint, and bitters.

3. Stir about 30 seconds, or until well-chilled.

4. Strain into a chilled cocktail glass.

5. Add garnish.

ARNAUD'S SPECIAL

Arnaud's Restaurant is a staple of the New Orleans dining scene, having opened in 1918. It is still going strong today. Off to one side of the restaurant, you'll find the French 75 Bar, managed by head bartender Chris Hannah. Mr. Hannah is a fine barman who has not only put his own stamp on such classics as the French 75 and the Sazerac but has also created many drinks of his own.

The Arnauld Special is not, however, one of Hannah's originals. Instead, it's a signature drink from earlier in Arnauld's history, when it was the house drink in the 1940s. It's a simple drink of Scotch, Dubonnet Rouge, and orange bitters—similar to a Rob Roy and yet also somehow very different. In his book *Vintage Spirits and Forgotten Cocktails*, Ted "Dr. Cocktail" Haigh suggests using Johnnie Walker Red for its smoky character. And I can't argue with Doc.

INGREDIENTS

2 ounces blended Scotch whisky

1 ounce Dubonnet Rouge

3 dashes orange bitters

Orange peel, for garnish

PROCEDURE

1. Fill a mixing glass ⅔ full of ice.

2. Add Scotch, Dubonet, and bitters.

3. Stir about 30 seconds, or until well-chilled.

4. Strain into a chilled cocktail glass.

5. Add garnish.

DERBY

Cocktail people really love horse racing, and horse racing aficionados really love cocktails. The mint julep, of course, is the drink of choice at the Kentucky Derby; the Preakness cocktail appears on page 184 of this book; and the Belmont Stakes have inspired not one, but three official cocktails: the vodka-based White Carnation, the Belmont Breeze, and the Belmont Jewel.

INGREDIENTS

1 ounce bourbon whiskey

½ ounce sweet vermouth

½ ounce orange curaçao

¾ ounce lime juice

PROCEDURE

1. Pour whiskey, vermouth, curaçao, and lime juice into a chilled mixing glass.

2. Add enough cracked ice to fill mixing glass about ⅔ full.

3. Stir about 30 seconds, or until well-chilled.

4. Strain into a chilled cocktail glass.

2000–Today

COCKTAIL RENAISSANCE, OR THE
SECOND GOLDEN AGE OF THE COCKTAIL

BARDSTOWN

The Bardstown cocktail is the creation of Andrew Friedman, owner of Liberty Bar in Seattle. It is, however, named after Bardstown, Kentucky, where Heaven Hill Distilleries was born. Heaven Hill is the current owner of the Rittenhouse brand of rye whiskey, a robust bonded whiskey that's popular with modern bartenders. This drink has been on the menu at Liberty for five or six years. Despite dozens of menu changes, this drink has remained one of Liberty's top sellers.

INGREDIENTS

1½ ounces **Rittenhouse Rye**

1 ounce **Laird's Apple Brandy 100 proof**

¼ ounce **Cointreau**

2 dashes **Angostura orange bitters**

Orange peel, for garnish

PROCEDURE

1. Pour rye, brandy, Cointreau, and bitters into a chilled mixing glass.

2. Add enough cracked ice to fill mixing glass about ⅔ full.

3. Stir about 30 seconds, or until well-chilled.

4. Strain into a chilled cocktail glass.

5. Squeeze the orange peel over the surface of the glass, rub the rim with the peel, and drop the peel into the glass.

JAPANESE GARDNER

Also from Seattle's Liberty Bar, this drink is by Keith Waldbauer and Andrew Friedman. It is named after Gardner Dunn, brand ambassador for Suntory.

INGREDIENTS

2 ounces Suntory Yamazaki 12-year-old Japanese whisky

½ ounce lemon juice

¼ ounce apricot liqueur

¼ ounce simple syrup

2 dashes Peychaud's Bitters

Small edible flower, for garnish

PROCEDURE

1. Pour whisky, lemon juice, apricot liqueur, simple syrup, and bitters into a chilled mixing glass.

2. Add enough cracked ice to fill mixing glass about ⅔ full.

3. Stir about 30 seconds, or until well-chilled.

4. Strain into old-fashioned glass. Add one large ice cube.

5. Add garnish.

WARD CLEAVER

I came up with this variation on a Ward Eight cocktail for an event called Mixology Monday, in which cocktail writers and bloggers share new and classic recipes on a given theme. Way back in late 2008, the theme was spice, and so I chose to infuse some rye whiskey with nuts and spices. The infusion makes more rye than you'll need for one cocktail. Save the rest for another time, or make more than one drink!

FOR THE INFUSION

¼ cup walnuts

1 stick cinnamon

1 teaspoon black peppercorns
(*Do not crush or grind the pepper, or you'll end up with a too-peppery infusion.*)

1 tablespoon lemon zest

1 cup Rittenhouse rye

FOR THE COCKTAIL

2 ounces infused rye

¾ ounce lemon juice

½ ounce grenadine

1 dash Angostura bitters

TO MAKE THE INFUSION

1. Add all ingredients to a jar with a capacity of at least 2 cups.

2. Place in a dark part of your kitchen for three days, shaking the jar every day.

TO MAKE THE COCKTAIL

1. Shake all ingredients in an ice-filled shaker.

2. Strain into a chilled cocktail glass.

RED HOOK

In the first decade of the 21st century, as the Brooklyn cocktail neared its centennial, bartenders started tinkering with the Brooklyn formula. They were soon creating new drinks and naming them for Brooklyn neighborhoods. The Red Hook cocktail keeps the Brooklyn's maraschino, drops the Amer Picon substitute, and uses Punt e Mes, a sweet vermouth known for its slightly bitter, herbal quality.

Red Hook is a gentrifying, but formerly industrial and maritime, neighborhood in western Brooklyn. The film *On the Waterfront*, though set in Hoboken, New Jersey, is evocative of the past of shipping neighborhoods such as Red Hook.

INGREDIENTS

2 ounces rye whiskey

½ ounce maraschino liqueur

½ ounce Punt e Mes

Cocktail cherry, for garnish

PROCEDURE

1. Fill a mixing glass ⅔ full of ice.

2. Add whiskey, maraschino liqueur, and Punt e Mes.

3. Stir about 30 seconds, or until well-chilled.

4. Strain into a chilled cocktail glass.

5. Add garnish.

GREENPOINT

The Greenpoint is another Brooklyn variant named for a neighborhood in the borough. The Greenpoint cocktail drops the Brooklyn's maraschino and the Amer Picon substitute, and uses herbal, spicy yellow Chartreuse.

Greenpoint is the northernmost neighborhood in Brooklyn. Like Red Hook, it was formerly industrial and maritime, but now the gentrification of Williamsburg, to its south, is spilling over into the area.

INGREDIENTS

2 ounces rye whiskey

1 ounce sweet vermouth

1 teaspoon yellow Chartreuse

1 dash Angostura bitters

Lemon peel, for garnish

PROCEDURE

1. Fill a mixing glass ⅔ full of ice.

2. Add whiskey, vermouth, Chartreuse, and bitters.

3. Stir about 30 seconds, or until well-chilled.

4. Strain into a chilled cocktail glass.

5. Squeeze the lemon peel over the surface of the glass, rub the rim with the peel, and drop the peel into the glass.

PENICILLIN

Some drinks are Prohibition-era classics; some are drinks that *seem* like they should be Prohibition-era classics. The Penicillin is the latter. It has a name that implies it's been around for decades, and it has a recipe that uses old-school ingredients, such as Scotch and ginger. But the Penicillin is a modern-day classic, invented a few years ago by Sam Ross at Milk & Honey in Manhattan. It's a rewarding and complex drink that's perfect for a cold night.

INGREDIENTS

3 slices fresh ginger

2 ounces blended Scotch whisky (I suggest The Famous Grouse)

¾ ounce lemon juice

¾ ounce Honey Syrup (see recipe, page 205)

¼ ounce peaty Islay single malt Scotch whisky (I suggest Laphroiag)

PROCEDURE

1. Muddle the fresh ginger in the bottom of a cocktail shaker until it's smashed. Add blended Scotch, lemon juice, and Honey Syrup.

2. Fill shaker with ice and shake for about 30 seconds, or until well chilled.

3. Double strain (see page 87) into an ice-filled rocks glass. Float the Islay Scotch over the back of a bar spoon atop the drink.

SEELBOCK

An example of what you can do with a little creativity and a willingness to tweak a classic, the Seelbock is my beer-topped variation on the Seelbach cocktail (page 146). The beer version uses rye in place of bourbon, lemon bitters in place of Peychaud's, and a German bock beer—a kind of strong lager—in place of champagne. The bock has a wheatiness that works well with whiskey. The bright citrus flavors of the lemon bitters and Cointreau make this a refreshing summer drink.

INGREDIENTS

1½ ounces rye whiskey

½ ounce Cointreau

¼ ounce lemon bitters

2 dashes Angostura bitters

4–5 ounces bock beer

Lemon twist, for garnish

PROCEDURE

1. In a mixing glass filled with ice, stir rye, Cointreau, and both bitters.

2. Strain into champagne flute and top with beer.

3. Squeeze the lemon peel over the surface of the glass, rub the rim with the peel, and drop the peel into the glass.

HAIKU D'ETAT

From The Alembic bar in San Francisco, comes this delicate and herbal cocktail—one of the few in this book that features Japanese whisky. If you can't find Akashi White Oak, any unpeated Japanese whisky will do. Try Yamazaki 12 Year Old, for example.

Here at The Alembic, we like to take poetic license with our cocktails. Akashi White Oak Japanese whisky, shiso, honey, citrus, and a wash of Laphroaig 10-year come together to create a unique and elegant rhythm.
—Larry Piaskowy, bartender at The Alembic

INGREDIENTS

Few dashes Laphroaig

2 ounces Akashi White Oak blended Japanese whisky

½ ounce Honey Shiso Syrup (see recipe, page 211)

¼ ounce orange juice

¼ ounce lime juice

1 dash celery bitters

1 shiso leaf

Grapefruit peel, for garnish

PROCEDURE

1. Rinse coupe glass with Laphroaig, and let it sit with an ice cube or two while you prepare the cocktail, and then discard.

2. Add remaining ingredients, except garnish, into an ice-filled cocktail shaker. Shake for about 15 seconds to chill and combine ingredients.

3. Double strain into prepared coupe.

4. Squeeze grapefruit peel over the surface of the drink, rub it around the rim of the glass, and discard.

HONEY CAKE

Perhaps it's fitting that a kosher-certified rye would form the basis of a drink that is inspired by a Jewish tradition of serving honey cakes at holidays. This recipe comes from Emily Landsman, brand ambassador for Catoctin Creek.

INGREDIENTS

½ teaspoon crushed fall spices, such as cinnamon, star anise, clove, allspice, etc.

3 ounces Catoctin Creek Roundstone Rye whiskey

2 ounces freshly squeezed orange juice

1 ounce Honey Syrup (see recipe, page 205)

Orange peel, for garnish

PROCEDURE

1. Stir spices into whiskey and allow the mixture to sit for several hours or overnight to infuse. Strain whiskey through a strainer with a coffee filter to remove the spices.

2. Add spiced whiskey, juice, and Honey Syrup to a cocktail shaker with several pieces of ice. Shake for 10 to 15 seconds. Strain into a chilled coupe glass.

3. Garnish with orange peel, twisting before you toss it into the drink to release oils in the peel.

Chapter 5

MIXER RECIPES

You can't make good cocktails without high-quality syrups and garnishes on hand. Although you can find some commercial products that are great in cocktails, most of these ingredients are a snap to make at home. In this chapter, I'll provide recipes for making those ingredients in your own kitchen.

GINGER SYRUP

Used in the Cablegram (page 159) and Presbyterian (page 204).

INGREDIENTS

4 ounces fresh ginger, unpeeled

2 cups water

1 cup sugar

PROCEDURE

1. Slice ginger as thinly as you can, and then roughly chop it into smaller pieces.

2. Place ginger, water, and sugar in a small, heavy saucepan over medium-low heat. Simmer for 30 minutes.

3. Strain through a sieve and then let cool to room temperature. The syrup will stay fresh in the refrigerator for two weeks.

HONEY SYRUP

Honey makes a lovely cocktail sweetener, adding the subtle flavors of flowers or fruit to a drink without using actual flowers or fruit. Working with honey in cocktails is simple, but because honey is too thick to blend easily into a cold cocktail, you first need to make a syrup. The process is so simple that you barely need a recipe, though I'll provide one anyway.

I suggest clover honey here because its flavor is light, mildly sweet, and subtly floral.

INGREDIENTS

½ **cup clover honey**

½ **cup water**

PROCEDURE

1. Add honey and water to a small saucepan on low heat. Cook until the honey melts into the water.

2. Bottle, cap, and store in the refrigerator for two weeks. The syrup shouldn't separate in the fridge, but it doesn't hurt to shake before using.

RASPBERRY SYRUP

Formerly a very common cocktail ingredient, raspberry syrup is due for a renaissance in the bar world. It's easy to make and, if you have more than you need for drinks, it's great in iced tea or lemonade.

INGREDIENTS

6 cups raspberries

¾ cup sugar

½ cup water

PROCEDURE

1. Combine raspberries, sugar, and water in a medium saucepan over medium-high heat. Cook until raspberries break down and release their juice.

2. Remove from heat; let stand for at least 15 minutes. Strain through a sieve, pressing down on solids to extract as much liquid as possible.

3. Bottle and refrigerate.

GRENADINE

Grenadine is a cocktail syrup named after the French word for pomegranate, *grenade*. (I suppose an actual hand grenade does look a little bit like a pomegranate, if you squint.) You can buy grenadine, but it's hard to find products that are all natural; a lot of the commercial stuff is artificially flavored and colored. It's super easy to make, though. A short blast of heat on the stovetop and some stirring will do the trick. The flavor and aroma of freshly made grenadine are so appealingly bright and fruity that you'll fall in love with it immediately.

The recipe calls for pomegranate molasses and orange flower water, both of which you can find at a Mediterranean grocery or online. They add great depth of flavor to the grenadine, and though you can make the syrup without them, you'll be seriously missing out. The vodka is here to preserve the grenadine. If you're planning to use it all within a month, you can skip the vodka.

(Adapted from Jeffrey Morgenthaler's *The Bar Book*.)

INGREDIENTS

2 cups 100 percent pomegranate juice (I like POM Wonderful)

2 cups cane sugar

2 ounces pomegranate molasses

1 teaspoon orange flower water

1 ounce 100 proof vodka

PROCEDURE

1. In a small saucepan, heat the juice until it's just hot enough to dissolve the other ingredients. Heating it hotter than this will cook away the fresh, bright flavors of the juice, so be gentle.

2. Add other ingredients and stir to dissolve.

3. When the grenadine is cool, bottle it and store in the refrigerator until you're ready to use it.

COCKTAIL CHERRIES

Finding a good cocktail cherry is a difficult task. The ones you can get in most supermarkets are garbage—cherries bleached and brined in a chemical bath, dyed neon colors, and doused in sugar syrup. Maybe your kids will eat them, but I think they have no place in a cocktail.

A couple of companies make an old-school cocktail cherry. (Luxardo is the easiest to find.) The cocktail cherry arose in Europe, which has a long and lovely history of preserving fruit in liqueur or brandy. Maraschino cherries arose in a coastal region of what is now Croatia. The region's native Marasca cherries are smaller and firmer than most varieties grown in the States.

Historically, maraschino cherries were sort of a Russian nesting doll of cherry flavor. First, maraschino liqueur would be distilled from Marasca cherries. Then another batch of Marasca cherries would be steeped in that liqueur, to preserve and flavor the cherries. Maraschino tastes oddly more almond-like than it does cherry. But that's okay: Nutty flavors are a great addition to whiskey cocktails.

½ **pound cherries**

¼ **cup water**

½ **cup turbinado sugar**

½ **cup cherry juice (see
recipe above)**

½ **teaspoon real vanilla
extract**

¼ **teaspoon freshly
ground nutmeg**

Pinch of salt

1 cup maraschino liqueur

1 pound cherries

1. Take ½ pound cherries, stem and pit them, and purée them in a blender with ¼ cup water. Strain the juice through a fine-mesh strainer to remove skins and other solids.

1. In a medium saucepan, combine sugar, cherry juice, vanilla extract, nutmeg, and salt. Bring to a low simmer. Simmer, stirring until sugar is fully dissolved.

2. Remove saucepan from heat. Add maraschino liqueur, and stir to combine.

3. Add 1 pound cherries and stir until coated with syrup.

4. Pour into clean canning jars. Let cool to room temperature and then refrigerate overnight before serving. They'll stay good for months in the refrigerator.

SIMPLE SYRUP

One funny thing about making cocktails, and also about writing about them, is that simple syrup isn't all that simple. Read bar menus, cocktail blogs, or other cocktail books, and you'll see mentions of *rich simple syrup*, *2:1 simple syrup*, *1:1 simple syrup*, *gum/gomme syrup*, and other esoterica. *Rich simple syrup* sometimes refers to simple syrup made with a brown sugar, such as turbinado, that produces a richer-tasting syrup as compared to white sugar concoctions. But *rich simple syrup* also sometimes means a syrup made of two parts sugar to one part water, which is also known as *2:1 simple syrup*. It can be confusing.

Not for us, though. Most of the recipes in this book that require simple syrup require only a 1:1 sugar:water ratio. And it's easy to make. For a 2:1 simple syrup, as used in the Japanese Gardner (page 193), simply double the amount of sugar.

INGREDIENTS

½ **cup sugar**

½ **cup water**

PROCEDURE

1. In a small saucepan, combine sugar and water and simmer over low heat until sugar dissolves.

2. Let cool and bottle. Store it in the refrigerator, and try to use it within a few weeks, after which point, it will spoil.

MINT SYRUP

To make this mint syrup (or minted simple syrup), make a simple syrup as instructed on page 210 and, while the syrup cools, add ¼ cup tightly packed mint leaves. Let it steep for 15 minutes, then strain the syrup into a clean jar. Store in the refrigerator for no longer than two weeks.

HONEY SHISO SYRUP

Shiso is an Asian herb in the mint family. To make this mint syrup (or minted simple syrup), make Honey Syrup as instructed on page 205 and, while the syrup cools, add ¼ cup tightly packed shiso leaves. Let it steep for 15 minutes, then strain the syrup into a clean jar. Store in the refrigerator for no longer than two weeks.

INDEX

Note: Italicized pages refer to recipe photos.

A

Abricot du Roussillon, in The
    Acadien, 93
absinthe
    Cocktail à la Louisiane, 188
    Modern Cocktail #1, 143
    Modern Cocktail #2, 144
    Morning Glory Cocktail,
      116–17
    Morning Glory Fizz, 118
    Remember the Maine, 164
    Sazerac, 136–37
The Acadien, 93
age statements, 32
aging process
    age statements, 32
    for bourbon, 57–58, 62–63
    factors affecting, 31–32
    oak barrels and, 26
    used whiskey barrels and, 30–31
    See also unaged whiskey
alcohol distillation, 23–25
Algonquin, *172*, 173
allspice dram, in Lion's Tail, 170
amaretto liqueur, in Godfather,
    178–79
Amaro CioCiaro
    Brooklyn, 139
    Creole Cocktail, 161
American craft whiskeys, 66–67
aperatifs. *See specific aperatifs*
apple brandy, in Bardstown, 192
applejack, in Diamondback, 174
apricot(s)
    liqueur, in Japanese Gardner, 193
    Rock and Rye, 132–33
Arnaud's Special, 189

B

Bar Book, The (Morgenthaler), 87,
    207

Bardstown, 192
barley, as whiskey grain, 19
barrels, making (cooperage), 26–31
    See also casks; oak barrels
batching and blending, 32–36
beer
    affinity with whiskey, 15
    in Seelbock, 199
Bénédictine liqueur
    Bobby Burns, 140–41
    Cocktail à la Louisiane, 188
    Creole Cocktail, 161
    Monte Carlo, 182–83
    Preakness, 184–85
    Vieux Carré, 187
blended Scotch whisky
    Cameron's Kick, 160
    described, 32, 34, 36
    Little More Complex
      Presbyterian, 127
    Modern Cocktail #1, 143
    Morning Glory Fizz, 118
    Prince Edward, 129
    Ridiculously Simple
      Presbyterian
    127
blended whiskey
    Bobby Burns, 140–41
    described, 18, 32, 36
    Leatherneck, 176–77
blending and batching, 32–36
Blinker, 154
Blood and Sand, 155
Bobby Burns, *140*, 141
bottled-in-bond bourbon, 64
Boulevardier, 156, *157*
Bourbon, Strange (Cowdery), 26
bourbon recipes
    Cherry Bounce, 96–97
    Classic Manhattan, 121
    Derby, 190

Dry Manhattan, 122
Fanciulli, 142
Fancy Whiskey Cocktail, 114
Horse's Neck, 128
Lion's Tail, 170
Mint Julep, 102–4
Mother-in-Law, 175
Perfect Manhattan, 122
Seelbach, 146–47
Stone Fence, 98
Whiskey Cocktail, 113
Whiskey Crusta, 108
Whiskey Smash, 106–7
Whiskey Sour, 109
bourbon whiskey
    aging of, 57–58, 62–63
    defined, 61
    history of, 56–61
    making, 61
    mixing with, 63–64
    name origin of, 62
    sour mash process, 63
    wheat whiskey, 63
Brooklyn, 139
Brown-Forman, 28–29

C

Cablegram, *158*, 159
Cameron's Kick, 160
Campari
    Boulevardier, 156–57
    Old Pal, 162
Canadian Club, 69
Canadian whisky
    aging of, 69
    blended, 34
    defined, 68
    grains used in, 20
    history of, 68
    making, 68–69
    mixing with, 69

Canadian whisky recipes
  The Acadien, 93
  Toronto, 168–69
caramel coloring, note on, 26
casks
  Scotch whisky and, 48–49
  sherry casks, aging in, 30, 47, 49
  See also oak barrels
champagne, in Prince of Wales, 134
charring/toasting barrels, 29, 57
Chartreuse
  Diamondback, 174
  Greenpoint, 197
  Tipperary, 145
cherries
  Cherry Bounce, 96–97
  Cocktail Cherries, 208–9
  liqueur, in Blood and Sand, 155
  liqueur, in Remember the Maine, 164
cider, hard, in Stone Fence, 98
citrus
  citrus twists, 88
  juicing, 91
  organic vs. conventional, 90–91
  See also grapefruit; orange(s)
Cocktail à la Louisiane, 188
Cocktail Cherries, 208–9
cocktail recipes. See whisky cocktails
cocktails, 75–93
  citrus for, 79, 88, 90–91
  creating, 92–93
  egg whites, frothing, 89–90
  equipment for, 75–79
  flavor rinsing, 91–92
  glassware for, 79–80
  mixing techniques, described, 81
  muddling technique, 88–89
  origins of, 124
  stirring and shaking techniques, 81–85, 89–90
  straining cocktails, 85–87
coffee, in Irish Coffee, 180–81
cognac
  Morning Glory Cocktail, 116–17
  Prescription Julep, 110–11
  Twelve Mile Limit, 165
  Vieux Carré, 187

Cointreau
  Bardstown, 192
  Morning Glory Cocktail, 116–17
  Mother-in-Law, 175
  Police Gazette Cocktail, 150–51
  Seelbach, 146–47
  Seelbock, 199
column stills, 24–25
cooperage (barrel making), 26–31
corn, as whiskey grain, 20, 61
craft whiskeys, American, 66–67
Creole Cocktail, 161
Crowgey, Henry, 62
curaçao
  Derby, 190
  Leatherneck, 176–77
  Whiskey Crusta, 108

D
Derby, 190
Diageo, 34
Diamondback, 174
distillation, 23–25
distilleries. See specific distilleries
Drambuie
  Bobby Burns, 140–41
  Prince Edward, 129
  Rusty Nail, 186
dry shake technique, 90–91
Dubonnet Rouge, in Arnaud's Special, 189

E
Elk's Fizz, 152
equipment for cocktails, 75–79
evaporation, 31

F
Fanciulli, 142
Fancy Whiskey Cocktail, 114
fermentation, 21–22
Fernet-Branca
  Fanciulli, 142
  Toronto, 168–69
flavor
  charring process and, 57
  factors affecting, 11–12, 33
  oak barrels and, 26
flavoring grains, 20
flavor rinses, 91–92
Four Roses distillery, 22–23

G
garnishes
  Cocktail Cherries, 208–9
ginger, in Penicillin, 198
ginger beer
  Horse's Neck, 128
  Mamie Taylor, 148–49
Ginger Syrup, 204
Glaser, John, 37
glassware, 79–80
Godfather, 178, 179
grain, as whiskey ingredient, 15–16, 18–20
grain whiskey, described, 17–18
Grand Marnier, in Fancy Whiskey Cocktail, 114
grapefruit juice, in Blinker, 154
Greenpoint, 197
Grenadine, 207

H
Haiku d'Etat, 200
historic cocktails
  first whiskey cocktails, 96–111
  Golden Age (1860-1899), 112–37
  pre-Prohibition (1900-1920), 138–52
  Prohibition-era (1920-1933), 153–70
  post-Prohibition (1933-1999), 171–90
  Renaissance, or second Golden Age (2000-today), 191–201
Honey Cake, 201
Honey Shiso Syrup, 211
Honey Syrup, 205
Horse's Neck, 128
hybrid stills, 25

I
ice trade, 101
Imbibe! (Wondrich), 99, 105, 117
Improved Whiskey Cocktail, 115
Independent Stave Company, 28, 31
international whiskey, 41–73
  American craft whiskeys, 66–67
  bourbon whiskey, 56–64
  Canadian whisky, 68–69
  Irish whiskey, 42–45
  Japanese whisky, 69–72

international whiskey (*continued*)
  maker profile, 53–55
  rye whiskey, 50–52
  Scotch whiskey, 45–50
  Tennessee whiskey, 65–66
  world whiskies, 72–73
Irish Coffee, 180–81
Irish whiskey
  blended, 34
  defined, 44
  history of, 42–44
  making, 44
  mixing with, 45
  single malt whiskey, 44
  single pot still whiskey, 18, 24,
    44–45
Irish whiskey recipes
  Cameron's Kick, 160
  Irish Coffee, 180–81
  Paddy, 163
  Tipperary, 145

J

Jack Daniel's, 29, 65, 66
Japanese Gardner, 193
Japanese whisky
  blended, 34
  defined, 71
  history of, 69–70
  making, 71–72
  mixing with, 72
Japanese whisky recipes
  Haiku d'Etat, 200
  Japanese Gardner, 193
Jim Beam, 22, 56, 61, 64, 70
Johnnie Walker, 34, 71

K

Kentucky
  Bourbon County, 62
  bourbon made in, 57–59

L

Leatherneck, *176*, 177
lemons. *See* citrus
Lillet Blanc, in Prince Edward, 129
limes. *See* citrus
Lion's Tail, 170
liqueurs. *See specific liqueurs*
Little More Complex
  Presbyterian, 127
Louisiane, Cocktail à la, 188

M

maker profiles, 37, 53–55
Maker's Mark, 31, 61, 63, 70
making whiskey, overview of,
  15–17
malted grains, 19–20
malt whiskey
  compared to beer, 15
  described, 17
Mamie Taylor, *148*, 149
Manhattan
  about, 120
  Classic, 121
  Dry, 122
  Perfect, 122
  variations of, 130–31, 163,
    182–83
maple syrup liqueur, in The Aca-
  dien, 93
maraschino liqueur
  Brooklyn, 139
  Cocktail Cherries, 208–9
  Improved Whiskey Cocktail,
    115
  Police Gazette Cocktail, 150–51
  Prince of Wales, 134
  Red Hook, 196
Maryland rye, 51–52
mashing process, 21
mint
  Mint Julep, 102, 103–4
  Whiskey Smash, 106–7
Mint Syrup, 211
  See also Honey Shiso Syrup
mixer recipes
  Cocktail Cherries, 208–9
  Ginger Syrup, 204
  Grenadine, 207
  Honey Shiso Syrup, 211
  Honey Syrup, 205
  Mint Syrup, 211
  Raspberry syrup, 206
  Simple Syrup, 210
mixing techniques, 81–87
mixing with whiskey. *See under
  specific whiskey types*
Modern Cocktail #1, 143
Modern Cocktail #2, 144
Monongahela rye, 51, 52
Monte Carlo, 83, *182*
moonshine, 38–39
Morning Glory Cocktail, *116*, 117

Morning Glory Fizz, 118
Mote, Lauren, 92–93
Mother-in-Law, 175
muddling technique, 88–89

N

New York Sour, 119

O

oak barrels
  American whiskey, 26
  bourbon, 62–63
  charred oak, 29, 57
  making (cooperage), 26–31
  rye whiskey, 52
  Scotch whisky, 49
Old-Fashioned, 123–25
  variations of, 113, 132–33,
    168–69, 187
Old Pal, 162
orange(s)
  Blood and Sand, 155
  Haiku d'Etat, 200
  Honey Cake, 201
  liqueur, in Fancy Whiskey
    Cocktail, 114
  Rock and Rye, 132–33
  Ward Eight, 135
  Whiskey Cobbler, 105
orgeat syrup, in Cameron's Kick,
  160
origin of whiskey, 41

P

Paddy, 163
peated whiskeys, 19–20
Penicillin, 198
pineapple
  Algonquin, 172–73
  Prince of Wales, 134
Police Gazette Cocktail, 150, *151*
pomegranate, in Grenadine, 207
port, ruby, in Elks' Fizz, 52
pot stills, 23–24
Preakness, 184, *185*
Presbyterian, *126*, 127
Prescription Julep, *110*, 111
Prince Edward, 129
Prince of Wales, 134
Prohibition, 43, 48, 60, 65
Prohibition–era cocktails. *See
  cocktails, Prohibition–era*

proof of whiskey
  bourbon, 61, 63–64
  Canadian whisky, 68
  laws regulating, 25, 61
  Tennessee whiskey, 66

R

Raspberry Syrup, 206
Red Hook, 196
Remember the Maine, 164
Renaissance cocktails. *See*
  cocktails, Golden Age,
  2000–today
Ridiculously Simple Presbyterian,
  127
Rittenhouse, 52, 60
Rob Roy, *130*, 131
Rock and Rye, 132–33
rum
  Modern Cocktail #1, 143
  Prescription Julep, 110–11
  Twelve Mile Limit, 165
Rusty Nail, 186
rye, as whiskey grain, 20
rye whiskey
  defined, 52
  history of, 50–51
  making, 52
  mixing with, 52
rye whiskey recipes
  The Acadien, 93
  Algonquin, 173
  Blinker, 154
  Boulevardier, 156–57
  Cablegram, 158–59
  Cocktail à la Louisiane, 188
  Creole Cocktail, 161
  Diamondback, 174
  Elks' Fizz, 152
  Fancy Whiskey Cocktail, 114
  Greenpoint, 197
  Honey Cake, 201
  Horse's Neck, 128
  Improved Whiskey Cocktail,
  115
  New York Sour, 119
  Old Pal, 162
  Police Gazette Cocktail, 150–51
  Preakness, 184–85
  Prince of Wales, 134
  Red Hook, 196
  Remember the Maine, 164

Sazerac, 136–37
Scofflaw, 166–67
Seelbock, 199
Stone Fence, 98
Twelve Mile Limit, 165
Vieux Carré, 187
Ward Eight, 135
Whiskey Cocktail, 113
rye whiskey recipes, high proof
  Bardstown, 192
  Brooklyn, 139
  Classic Manhattan, 121
  Dry Manhattan, 122
  Mint Julep, 103–4
  Monte Carlo, 182–83
  Morning Glory Cocktail,
  116–17
  Perfect Manhattan, 122
  Rock and Rye, 132–33
  Toronto, 168–69
  Ward Cleaver, 194–95
  Whiskey Cobbler, 105
  See also rye whiskey recipes

S

Sazerac
  flavor rinse for, 91
  recipe for, 136–37
  serving, 80
Scofflaw, *166*, 167
Scotch whisky
  defined, 48
  history of, 45–48
  making, 48–49
  mixing with, 49–50
  Scotch regions, 49
Scotch whisky recipes
  Arnaud's Special, 189
  Blood and Sand, 155
  Godfather, 178–79
  Mamie Taylor, 148–49
  Modern Cocktail #2, 144
  Penicillin, 198
  Rob Roy, 130–31
  Rusty Nail, 186
  See also blended Scotch whisky
Seelbach, 146, *147*
Seelbock, 199
shaking technique, cocktail, 83–85
sherry, in The Acadien, 93
Simple Syrup, 210
  variations of, 211

single grain whisky, defined, 36
single malt whiskey, defined, 34, 36
sloe gin, in Modern Cocktail #2,
  144
sour mash, 63
stills, types of, 23–25
stirring technique, cocktail, 82–83
Stone Fence, 98
straight whiskey, 18, 52
straining a cocktail, 85–87
Suntory, 70–71, 72, 193
syrups, recipes for. *See* mixer
  recipes

T

Tasting Whiskey (Bryson), 69
Tennessee whiskey, 65–66
Tipperary, 145
Toddy, 99
Torani Amer, in Mother-in-Law,
  175
Toronto, 168, *169*
Twelve Mile Limit, 165

U

unaged (white dog) whiskey, 38,
  39, 66

V

Veach, Michael, 62
vermouth, dry
  Dry Manhattan, 122
  Old Pal, 162
  Perfect Manhattan, 122
  Police Gazette Cocktail, 150–51
  Scofflaw, 166–67
  Vieux Carré, 187
vermouth, sweet
  Algonquin, 172–73
  Blood and Sand, 155
  Bobby Burns, 140–41
  Boulevardier, 156–57
  Brooklyn, 139
  Classic Manhattan, 121
  Creole Cocktail, 161
  Derby, 190
  Fanciulli, 142
  Greenpoint, 197
  Paddy, 163
  Preakness, 184–85
  Red Hook, 196
  Remember the Maine, 164

vermouth, sweet (*continued*)
  Rob Roy, 130–31
  Tipperary, 145
Vieux Carré, 187
Vintage Spirits and Forgotten Cocktails (Haigh), 189
Volstead Act, 60

W

Ward Cleaver, *194, 195*
Ward Eight, 135
warehouses, aging and, 31–33
Washington, George, 53–55
water, as whiskey element, 20–21
wheat whiskey, 63
whiskey, 15–39
  aging of, 26, 31–32
  blending and batching, 32–36
  categories of, 17–18
  defined, 15–16
  distillation process, 23–25
  fermentation process, 21–22
  ingredients for, 18–23, 25–31
  introduction to, 11–13
  maker profile, 37
  making, overview of, 15–17
  moonshine, 38–39
  origins of, 41
  proof of, 25, 61, 63–64, 66
  spelling of, 12–13
  See also specific types; whiskey
    cocktails
Whiskey Cobbler, 105
Whiskey Cocktail
  classic recipe, 113
  Fancy, 114
  Improved, 115
whiskey cocktails, first, 96–111
  Cherry Bounce, 96–97
  Mint Julep, 102–4
  Prescription Julep, 110–11
  Stone Fence, 98
  Toddy, 99
  Whiskey Cobbler, 105
  Whiskey Crusta, 108
  Whiskey Sling, 100
  Whiskey Smash, 106–7
  Whiskey Sour, 109
whiskey cocktails, Golden Age,
    112–37

Classic Manhattan, 121
Dry Manhattan, 122
Fancy Whiskey Cocktail, 114
Horse's Neck, 128
Improved Whiskey Cocktail,
    115
Little More Complex
    Presbyterian, 126
Morning Glory Cocktail,
    116–17
Morning Glory Fizz, 118
New York Sour, 119
Old-Fashioned, with Simple
    Syrup, 125
Old-Fashioned, with Sugar, 125
Perfect Manhattan, 122
Prince Edward, 129
Prince of Wales, 134
Ridiculously Simple
    Presbyterian, 126
Rob Roy, 130–31
Rock and Rye, 132–33
Sazerac, 136–37
Ward Eight, 135
Whiskey Cocktail, 113
whiskey cocktails, pre-Prohibition,
    138–52
  Bobby Burns, 140–41
  Brooklyn, 139
  Elk's Fizz, 152
  Fanciulli, 142
  Mamie Taylor, 148–49
  Modern Cocktail #1, 143
  Modern Cocktail #2, 144
  Police Gazette Cocktail,
    150–51
  Seelbach, 146–47
  Tipperary, 145
whiskey cocktails, Prohibition-era,
    153–70
  Blinker, 154
  Blood and Sand, 155
  Boulevardier, 156–57
  Cablegram, 158–59
  Cameron's Kick, 160
  Creole Cocktail, 161
  Lion's Tail, 170
  Old Pal, 162
  Paddy, 163
  Remember the Maine, 164

Scofflaw, 166–67
Toronto, 168–69
Twelve Mile Limit, 165
whiskey cocktails, post-
    Prohibition, 171–90
  Algonquin, 172–73
  Arnaud's Special, 189
  Cocktail à la Louisiane, 188
  Derby, 190
  Diamondback, 174
  Godfather, 178–79
  Irish Coffee, 180–81
  Leatherneck, 176–77
  Monte Carlo, 182–83
  Mother-in-Law, 175
  Preakness, 184–85
  Rusty Nail, 186
  Vieux Carré, 187
whiskey cocktails, Renaissance,
    191–201
  Bardstown, 192
  Greenpoint, 197
  Haiku d'Etat, 200
  Honey Cake, 201
  Japanese Gardner, 193
  Penicillin, 198
  Red Hook, 196
  Seelbock, 199
  Ward Cleaver, 194–95
Whiskey Crusta, 108
Whiskey Rebellion, 58
Whiskey Sling, 100
Whiskey Smash, 106, *107*
Whiskey Sour, 109
  variation of, 176–77
whisky/whiskey, spelling of,
    12–13
white dog (unaged) whiskey, 38,
    39, 66
Wild Turkey Distillery, 22, 25, 71
wine
  New York Sour, 119
  Seelbach, 146–47
wood, as whiskey ingredient,
    25–31
Woodford Reserve, 21–22, 34
world whiskies, 72–73

Y

yeast, 21–23